The Queen Of England

And

The Unknown Schoolboy:

Part 1

By Bob Crew

Paperback ISBN 978-1-80424-134-9
ePub ISBN 978-1-80424-135-6
PDF ISBN 978-1-80424-136-3

Published by MX Publishing
335 Princess Park Manor, Royal Drive,
London, N11 3GX
www.mxpublishing.com

Cover design by Brian Belanger

The fictional story that is told factionally in these pages is a true story inspired by real people and factual events before they get lost in the mists of time and it is written from memory, imagination and personal evidence-based experience, as well as from research and historical records that reportedly recorded these World War Two and later 1950s events at that time, informing the lives of those characterized in this narrative that is a story of how all this was understood or misunderstood at the time by an unknown schoolboy and his parents - from what they were given to understand and believe and what they thought about it all - and also from the prevailing research, some of the details of which may or may not have changed since that time. This is how hybrid works of faction are truthfully written and enjoyed fictionally and factually by those who rate this kind of literature.

A TWO-PART SEQUEL

This book is published as a two-part sequel – offering two bites at the cherry for readers (two for the price of one), the first part of which is for Christmas 2022 (the first Christmas without the late Queen Elizabeth II since her sad death earlier this year) and the second of which is for the New Year 2023 (the first New Year without her) – both parts of which can be ordered in book shops or online as an e-book now for delivery in time for Christmas (part-one) and the New Year (part-two).

Part-one of this book includes the first four chapters, with their preface and explanatory introduction, and as a two for the price of one Christmas and New Year publication – an economy of which the late Queen would almost certainly have approved! – this book is an ideal Christmas or New Year consumer gift for either of these festive occasions with which to celebrate our memories of her.

Part Two of this publication includes an insightful summary of the historical significance of a foregoing Christmas and New Year without the late Queen and the difference this has made.

Bob Crew – the author of this book – has written about British royals before, notably in his *Kate and The Commoner Queens* book and also in his *Gurkha Warriors* book in which the former Prince Charles, today's new King of England, is featured in an interview with him (the *Daily Express* newspaper said of this book ''Incisive, deadly and impossible to put down'').

Preface

Historical faction is the chosen genre for this book because there are important and valuable social, educational, political and royal truths to be explored in the story it has to tell, truths that cannot be particularly well explored or told otherwise by fact or fiction alone; and given the Netflix controversy invoked by *faction* regarding British royals in recent times, readers and/or critics of works of faction need to be crystal clear therefore about what the purposes of literary faction are and why it is a chosen genre for this publication that is written in the way in which it is written.

The argument in defence of literary faction needs to be understood, as does that of its critics who object to it.

With common consent, the chief, if not only reason, to write and/or read faction - fact turned into fiction - or to watch it on screen or stage, is to explore and discover an important and valuable truth or truths that pure fiction or pure fact (non-fiction) cannot discover on their own to very good effect, because neither uses the *imagination factually or as sufficiently* as faction does, and not least when it comes to history, with which to imagine and recreate the past and give it a big kiss of life with all the necessary facts.

Pure fiction uses the imagination without regard to too much or any fact - 'it only ever happens in fiction' - whilst pure factual writing has no truck with fiction at all. By contrast, faction is the hybrid alternative that, at its best, has the means with which to provide the best of both worlds (not the worst!).

1

Faction at its best is aimed for in these pages and, for example, the following is briefly how it works.

'Yes this happened in fact, but this is possibly why (fictionally imagined and created) and these were the most probable underlying emotional, social and psychological reasons for it to judge from the facts (fictionally imagined and created) or from the political and other fears that reportedly or triggered the alleged facts in question (fictionally imagined and created) that are all underlying reasons and fears that we need to consider and understand in order to better grasp the singular facts of the matter that have been handed down to us, and to get them into perspective, especially regarding matters of social justice or injustice (usually factual), the rights and wrongs of the matter (often debatable), the peculiar behavioural matters of different individuals in question (often debatable!), or perhaps the need for more or less compassion in relation to factual events and real-life people (debatable or not, as the case may be). Yes, those were the people, but how best to understand them and describe their inner natures, characters and personalities (??) in these telling respects, all of which need to be imagined (fictionally) and described and explained (factually).'

There is a fine overall balance to be struck and these are all truths that are important and valuable for obvious reasons, are they not?

And whilst we cannot bring all this vividly and humanely to life without imaginative fiction, we also need plenty of fact to go with it (non-fiction factual writing alone is not enough).

So we need to logically imagine (fictionally) and logically deduce and figure out (factually) how things probably or actually were *additional to the facts of the matter*, in order to get into those facts and discover *what more there is about them and to them*, and also to better comprehend them and their circumstances thereby; as we also

better-understand the hidden and not so hidden complexities of the characters and personalities of those involved, as opposed to the masks of their public persona.

Predictably, all this is a big ask and, in order to get this kind of writing and reading right, in works of historical and other kinds of faction, one must do this accurately and ethically (as this book certainly does) - making sure not to irresponsibly misrepresent, distort or defame the real-life factual people in the story, but to remain faithful to them and their possible/likely motivations, feelings and fears, and why they behaved or might have behaved as they did once upon a time, which may or may not have justified their matter of fact actions.

For example, 'this is what the factual people were very probably/obviously thinking because.......this is what they were apparently/evidently like and what exactly it is reasonable to suppose that they were thinking and saying or might have had good reason to think or say (or words to this effect) because ...... there was almost certainly/definitely an emotional impact (that the facts alone cannot convey on their own, hence the need for fictional-faction) as follows...... and so on.'

Because we cannot recreate and re-enact history and *bring it to life* in this way without the imaginative and creative intellectual power of fiction, we need to blend facts with fiction, or otherwise just accept what factual writing tells us about past events and people and nothing more than that,

3

that underpinned it – without a factual narrative imagining how matters must have felt or been, or what possibly motivated these matters with their underlying causes - or we can otherwise just accept what pure fiction does not tell us because it has no factual substance of any kind (just as pure factual writing does not tell us, likewise, because it has no imaginative fictional writing of any kind).

Of course, there are always differing opinions and debates about *more substance and less art* (in all the arts, not just in literature) and this can be a thought-provoking plus factor for faction, not a big black mark against it, and there is furthermore nothing to suggest that any of this is beyond the wit of ordinarily intelligent readers, viewers or critics to use their own judgements in these matters, according to their own intuition and personal experience of life and what makes sense to them from their own person experience and perspective.

Their literary comprehension and judgment of character has its own part to play, as does that of the writers of faction.

So, as we see, there's quite a lot to consider here!

A movable feast, no less.

There are also the purposes and rights of free and fair speculation and comment to consider (in a free and democratic world of freedom of speech and expression).

And, as we shall see in the following story, there is plenty to consider in all these respects about the late Queen of

England and her late husband and family and relatives after she first became the new Queen back in 1950s Britain when the protagonist of this story won her Coronation Prize.

INTRODUCTION

This is a story about a young working-class boy growing up in Britain under the social influence of the late Queen of England when she was Britain's new monarch back in the 1950s and it demonstrates the extraordinary reach of that influence when she first came to her throne, a totally different and dated kind of influence from the very modern influence that her memory still enjoys today more than half a century later for more than half the British population (according to the opinion polls), in addition to her global influence and not least in the United States where she has had a very considerable fan base.

This is also a story about the once upon a time Queen Elizabeth II Coronation Prize – mere book tokens – a prize that was awarded to school children back in the 1950s and how it influenced not more than a handful of crucially formative years in the life of one of the many unknown schoolboys (and girls) who won that prize and, in all probability, this is the first and only true story written about the late Queen of England from a once upon a time working-class point of view; showing how a former working-class schoolboy eventually became, as it happens, a professional member of the middle classes for his entire adult life, a decade or two later, living in a fashionable upper-middle-class prosperous suburb of London, not as a direct result of winning the Queen's not very grand royal prize, but with a little but notable help from it along the way, for sure – not practical help, but psychological and inspirational help.

For this reason, this is perhaps a ground-breaking little story, a story about not more than a few formative years (a mere handful) in a child's life that enables the late Queen's history and her country's social history to be better understood from a former working-class perspective rather than the usual royal and traditional perspectives of the usual royal correspondents, archivists and historians who generally represent the Queen of England and tell 'her' story, as they hand the tablets of stone down from on high at the top of the mountain.

But the stream of consciousness story told in these pages – flashing backwards and forwards in time - is not in any way the Queen of England's story, but the story of one of her subjects rather, and the story of the marginal but seriously notable difference that her Coronation Prize made to his life for the better – a life for the better that he would certainly have mastered and made better for himself without this prize, but a life in which, for all that and as things turned out, the Queen's prize had a pivotal role to play for the good, the significance of which was the very agreeable eye-opening power play that that the award of this prize represented – the power of royal influence socially and regionally right throughout the United Kingdom; the political and social aspects and implications of which make this a political story to some extent, but only in passing, because this is chiefly a non-political narrative about a 1950s unknown schoolboy and his family and school, not primarily a story about politics.

This is chiefly a story about psycho-dynamics and also language, how language is acquired and used, and how books are written.

With its flash-backs and flashes forward the story unfolds, regarding so many different aspects of history and points in time, and few if any other books about Queen Elizabeth II can claim the distinction of having a very different perspective to offer, from the bottom of the mountain looking up, rather than from the top looking down!

A work of literary/historical faction about the distant yet not so distant past, this is a story that brings back the atmospheric 'feel' and 'flavour' (the key role of faction) of those 1950s times, reminding us that if we do not *feel* the past and re-live and re-visit our past *feelingly from which we come*, then we are foreigners to it, and that nations and cultures that do not feel and re-visit/re-live their past, are very different from those that do (British royals understand this more than most, given that they and their governments and royalist armed forces so expertly architect the past and re-live it with passion and feeling).

Re-visiting/re-living the past, thanks to its royals, makes Britain in particular very different from other nations because, arguably, most others do not have an instant awareness of and ready *feel* for their pas times as those that regularly re-visit and re-live them, as Britain does annually; and this is not least because these other nations are not touched or moved in passing by their past in the same old-familiar and also old-fashioned ways of the past that are kept theatrically alive for people in Britain (in the theatres, places of worship, on the streets and in the parks where *God Save the Queen* pageantry and heraldry and worship has been in full swing in these places for decades in the United Kingdom, for as long as the longest memories can remember).

From whichever social part of the past we all come – and the past comes in many different shapes and shades of colour for all kinds of different people, latecomers and old-comers, does it not? – we are told by the opinion polls that more than half the British population has responded to this (with a passion, as we know).

Because in Britain the past is re-visited, re-lived and re-enacted by pageantry and ceremonial, and also with so many exhibitions and relics in this or that museum, by television and other films, and also in stage theatres – as well as in history books, poetry, obituaries and newspaper articles – it stands to reason that without all this in our cultural DNA, we cannot-not be readily familiar with or aware of our past (however superficially is neither here nor there) and we cannot-not re-visit it or re-live it and it feel it thereby, as we bump into our past at virtually every turn, and sniff it in the air we breathe in this refreshing and cathartic way (catharsis of this kind is arguably much more generally positive and not least for the ongoing cultural, moral, social, spiritual and mental good than the negative of having no catharsis at all).

Happily, we have all this in our British culture in spades, with which to live with/be reminded of our past in our present, always in the back or the forefront of our minds.

Revisiting and/or reliving the past in our minds is not such a difficult or complicated concept as it may sound, not for those that travel back in time with their eyes wide open, as opposed to only partly open (or perhaps even closed or with their heads in the sand!).

In my experience, by re-enacting and/or observing this with our eyes wide-open - when revisiting or remembering the past - we can and do soon get the hang of it and the swing and rhythm of it, with which to more clearly understand the cathartic significance and value of it.

There is nothing mystical or mysterious about any of this, but we do have to pay attention to detail if that detail is to fall or fit into place like bits of a jigsaw puzzle and become comprehensible and meaningful to us; a clear comprehension of which arguably enables us to better-understand and better-cope with the prognosis of the human condition in our continuing present and future (given that life is an inescapable three-part story of continuity and passing the baton from the past to the present and future whether we like it or realise it or not, as we move with the times and ahead of the times more maturely and knowingly as a direct result of confidently knowing or being aware of our past times and also how they have shaped and influenced us for good or ill, as is demonstrated in the pages of this book).

We have only to look at the long list of tyrants and other monumental undesirables that history has thrown at people in countries other than Britain in the absence of the aforementioned (typically British) *ongoing prognosis of the human condition* - that Britain has had so uniquely to its credit as a direct result of continually *re-living, re-learning and respecting its past and not forgetting it (but having instant re-call of it rather)* – in order to understand the present-day value of this for the good and its implications for the future.

And much of this is *thanks in particular to recreating the romance and fiction and real-life faction of the past in order to reflect all this* (the latter of which can of course sometimes be though-provokingly contentious and here's to it for that reason, because we all need to 'think' about what we feel in a free-thinking and grown-up society, do we not?).

The factional literature in this book is what the aforesaid cultural DNA and prognosis of the human condition is all about.

One can read stone-cold factual history books about our royal and other kinds of past, but it is my belief that only in the gentler and warmer climate of historical fiction or faction can one best *feel* and take the temperature of what the past was really 'like' and how it has shaped us for the better today, additional to the facts and events of past matters, such as what it was additionally like psychologically and mentally (with all that inner-thinking and reading between the lines and all that string pulling behind the scenes) – what it was like intellectually, emotionally, domestically, morally and socially, each and all of which of course impacts on history and the constituents of what that history was very probably/almost certainly *actually like,* and how it very probably felt for people in so many different ways.

But this is only one opinion among so many conflicting and contrasting others about the past and its literature that will chime with some readers but not with others – the opinion in favour of faction being that we can actually discover and get the feel of our history in feasible and plausible faction or fiction better than in purely factual literature – as and when the faction or fiction is intelligently feasible and plausible (and there's the rub!) – and this is because factual literature rarely if at all or sufficiently touches with sensitivity upon what the past was like *with regard to how it felt and why it felt,* so it does not give us that hand in the glove *feel* for or humanisation of our history that can make our present and future more rather than less humane.

One can best feel all this and have a much more subtle understanding of it from fiction/faction because the *Double-F* addresses this issue and suggests its possibilities to our imagination that facts and factual writing alone do not usually address or suggest, as they keep strictly to only what is or was known for sure about the past, end of story, without any literary inventions or feasible/plausible imaginings.

There is too often no second sense or second sight – excluding unnatural divine intervention, naturally! - or truly perceptive perception of these matters in purely factual books that are lacking in these respects. There is no *immersion* or *saturation* of feeling and, with an institution such as the British royal family – 'never explain never complain' (i.e. the power of silence and of being seen but not heard) – getting the feel of it without explanation from it (or with official misrepresentation by it!) is no easy task when writing about it (no wonder so many things go wrong, as the institution so often contradicts itself by complaining like mad that it is being misrepresented or misreported in the media and/or in works of fiction/faction, as a result of its reluctance or refusal to explain itself!).

Because faction and/or fiction goes probingly where facts do not go in this extra-curricular way (where angels fear to tread!), with much more immersion and saturation of feeling, it is by far the best way, in my view, of getting the feel of British royalty when being given the cold shoulder by it ('never explain')!

And it is this 'getting the feel' that is attempted in this (and other) works of literature.

Most factual stories in today's media about British royals – of which, as we know, there are a great many – are chiefly if not entirely about the royals themselves, gossipy and otherwise (their costumes and designer clothes etc), not about their subjects in relation to them as is the story in these pages, and not about the way in which their subjects' lives are/have been directly and/or indirectly shaped by them, which is what this unusual and presumably intriguing work of historically revealing faction in this book is all about, as 'the moving finger writes and having writ moves on.'

Once upon a time in the not too distant and not to near past – half a century and more ago – British royals shaped their subjects lives much less transparently and with less criticism and analysis than they receive today, as we shall see before we are though with this book that takes us down memory lane on a journey of social history in which we are powerfully reminded that the past really is another country (if not another planet!).

The life of the young Paul McCartney in Liverpool, for one, was influenced in those 1950s days by the Queen of England when he, also, was one of her unknown schoolboys (same as the protagonist in this book), before Paul became a pop singer and famous Beatle. He, too, was an unknown schoolboy who won a prize-winning essay about Britain's new queen on the scene (not that he features in this particular story).

We mostly recognise British royals today by the factual stories that we read about them in the media and how they respond to the crowds on their televised walkabouts – and also online when one or other of them weirdly plays strip poker with naked young women in a hotel suite (the mobile pics of which go viral!), whilst other royals have their controversial extra-marital and pre-marital sexual relations with women who are or are not under-aged – and many of these latter stories are stranger than fiction!

And we also watch British royals on television when they bravely risk their lives in battle, along with everybody else.

But in the work of faction in these pages we read about a very young 1950s Queen of England and some very different royals, as well as how her very different subjects related to her in much more innocent and gullible times that are now rapidly being lost in the mists of time (we read about the pluses and minuses of those times in this very human-interest story).

We read about a Queen that was known to her unknown subjects - who were so obviously seen and not heard in such a massively calculated and socially engineered way that they were generally complete strangers to her - while she was all too familiar to them (but in no way with them or of them), as she influenced their lives either directly or indirectly, or with the award of a prize, as explained in this story.

This is a work of faction for all who are interested in the literary device of faction and how it is written and why, interested in how books are written and read, how language is used, and also in Britain's social history and its changing face in the modern world, as well as the position of women in British society in the fairly recent but distant past (portrayed especially by the protagonist's mother, representative of millions of other women somewhat or exactly like her); and it is no exaggeration to say that there is very probably no other book about the late Queen Elizabeth II like this one, capturing how the queen was perceived and worshipped, at and from the grass roots once upon a time, perceived and worshipped very differently from how she was perceived and regarded much later on in her more recent reign before she died.

This is also a work that explores the workings of our thought processes and how they do or do not develop in young children en-route to the adult mind, the reasons that they do or do not develop, as well as being a work that explores the reading habits of pre and post-World-War-Two Britain.

Readers who can relate to and feel for the protagonist in this story – as I can certainly relate to and feel for him (as he appeals to my imagination, viewing him from afar and a distance, as I do, and with my knowledge of 1950s history of which I also have personal evidence-based experience) – those will be the readers that will no doubt enjoy this book more than those who cannot relate to such a person, given that it helps for a central character to be a *sympathetic character* for readers to be in sympathy with him or her (seeing as they have to keep company with a central character for the entire duration of a book).

But he is just one of several other factional characters in this fictional book (that were typical of their time in my opinion and also to my certain knowledge because I was there at the time to witness it all), so this is not just a one-man story or monologue or stream of consciousness (this is a shared stream of consciousness).

In addition to the singular authorial voice of the commentator there are the fictionalised voices of many others, each and all of whom are either reliable or unreliable narrators for one good reason or another that readers can judge for themselves, plausible or not, as the case may be, each and all of whom represent so many different and conflicting points of view, but all of whom were typical of their time and representative of how people were and why they thought as they thought.

There is a fascinating head master, a mother and father, a geography and other teachers, in addition to the commentary of an authorial voice in our ears (with which we must also keep company).

Whilst this is a fictional book because conversations, dialogues and situations are invented for this story to be imagined, told and explained (this is how these books are written - right? – there is no other way), there is nothing fictional about the well-remembered and personally witnessed factional characters and events in this perfectly true story, the art of which and the telling of which relies on fictional conversations and dialogues giving the past a kiss of life and bringing it and its characters back to life from the grave!

So!!

If all this makes sense (albeit laboriously!), or otherwise appeals to readers, having read this introduction, then hopefully they will read on and enjoy!

If not, they should ditch this book straight away, before it disappoints them even more.

Bob Crew
BA (Hons), MA, English Literature, University of London

The following is the brief timeline of this book:

1947: Princess Elizabeth of the House of Windsor Marries Her German Prince.

1952: She becomes Queen Elizabeth II of England at 25 years of age.

1953: She has her £4 million-plus televised Coronation in Westminster Abbey.

1954: Her Coronation Prize is Awarded to The Unknown Schoolboy in these pages who goes from his cloth-cap origins to a top-hat professional life, doing so on his own merit in the classroom and in the professional white-collar workplace.

Throughout her period of 1950s time – and thereafter – Elizabeth had the unfailing devotion and loyalty of the unknown schoolboy's mother and millions of others like her for reasons that become obvious when reading this book. She also had the respect of the schoolboy and his father and most of his school teachers.

....

The factual information woven into this work of true fiction/faction is verifiable in the history books and press reports of the period, and also in books of encyclopaedia, and because it is a work of true faction - most of the characters of whom are long gone - today's readers that can remember (or easily imagine) what was going on back then, really should resist the temptation to mistake or confuse anybody they know or knew or still know in real life, with the real-life and very true fictional/factional characters portrayed in these pages (other than the Queen of England and her royals, of course, as well as indisputably factually-known others, such as politicians and their like).

This is of course because real-life people with coincidental names are not necessarily or at all the same as fictionally invented 'characters' however similar they may appear to be.

CONTENTS

Chapter One: The Queen of England's 1954 Coronation Prize

The headmaster, a tall giant of a man of about forty, sat in his study, ready to receive a fourteen-year-old schoolboy whose name was Robert.

Called Jacko Jackson, this headmaster was a larger than life Welshman, who did not suffer fools gladly, or brook any disobedience or indiscipline from pupils, and although he was known as Jacko to other teachers and friends, he insisted on being addressed at all times as 'sir' by his pupils and as, Mr Jackson, by their parents. If any of the latter were remiss enough to take the liberty of calling him Jacko, he would soon tell them 'it's Mr Jackson to you and don't you forget it. I don't encourage informality with pupils or their parents.'

With no trace of a Welsh accent, Jacko spoke in the standard Oxford/BBC English of a typical officer and gentleman in the British royal navy.

Clearly spoken English with a standard or posh English accent was reckoned to be very important in Jacko Jackson's time when one could not get a superior or decent job with what was officially considered to be a socially inferior accent that was mispronounced or could not be clearly understood, and for this reason, many people seeking to self-improve their station in life took elocution lessons - or paid attention to speaking English and enunciating it as it was meant to be spoken - especially in the South and Southeast of England from where Robert came and took care to master the art of well-spoken English in order to make his way in life and get ahead, swiftly dropping his working-class 'country' accent, as did his mother to a large extent; but not his father who regularly dropped his aitches and forgot to pronounce so many other letters in the words that he spoke – doin,' thinkin' and all the rest, including 'E for he (it wasn't so much that people deliberately dropped their aitches and deliberately forgot to pronounce other letters in the alphabet, it was much more a matter of their never having known or been taught them them or got them right in the first place, so they had nothing to drop or forget!).

Robert's father – who left school at 11 years of age to become a boy soldier in the British Cavalry, like his father before him – even pronounced chimney as 'chimly,' whilst his mother regularly referred to children as 'going through a phrase,' rather than a phase, whilst his younger brother could not get the hang of saying anything, so repeatedly said 'any think,' instead!

To mention just a few of their illiterate mispronunciations that of course disqualified them for a goodly number of jobs and social circles.

It is not hard to understand the humiliation and embarrassment that went with speaking the language in this perverse way, humiliation for those that wanted to speak it correctly and be treated as equals, but not for those who could not care less and regarded their proudly ignorant and crude use of language as a V-Sign to the upper and middle classes.

Robert's father, mother and younger brother were in neither of these categories and, as for Robert himself, he avoided all this humiliation and embarrassment nonsense and also giving a V-Sign to the middle and upper classes, simply by doing what working-class others would not do – unlike Robert, they would not fall in line with all students of English and learn how to write, spell and speak the language correctly, regardless of class and no sweat (virtually everybody else in Robert's sector of the working-class failed or refused to do this, either because they could not be bothered, or because teachers could not be bothered with them, and not infrequently with good reason, as we shall see in this story!).

Yet Robert's father was a man of high intelligence regardless of his poor English as we shall see before we are though with this story.

Given that the first key to understanding and educations is of course language – reading and writing - those that spurned correct English inevitably condemned themselves to a lesser life work-wise and socially.

Robert took no elocution lessons but, at the same time, he took the sensible and honest to goodness view that the English language belonged to all the people who were free to speak it correctly if they preferred to do so regardless of their class, as he certainly wanted and intended to do - as no particular class, privileged or otherwise, had or has the copyright on the English tongue - and given that he had every intention of becoming an English Language and Literature scholar if at all possible, he exercised his right to speak the language properly and with nothing but respect for it; using it as he preferred to hear it and write it, so resisting a working-class 'country' accent that almost certainly would have come his way, had he not resisted and declined to speak English badly or in an ugly way that was popular where he lived.

Because he saw no reason why he should have to display his working-class 'country' accent like a badge of honour (or dishonour!!) in the class war that was intended for it, in his opinion, just because he was not born with a standard BBC/Oxford English accent (as the upper and most of the middle classes were), he flatly refused to speak with the working-class regional accent that was otherwise meant for him. So he intelligently dropped his local accent in favour of well-spoken English, and this got him into a lot of trouble with the children in his neighbourhood school and the street where he lived, as they ganged up on him and derided the 'superior' way that he spoke, which was not their way. Because they were stuck with accents they could not or would not discard, they said that it was unnatural and pretentious for him to 'fake' an unnatural accent (this often led to playground fights and street fights!), and for him to think (allegedly) that he was better than others by insisting on speaking (and writing) better than they chose to do or could not work out how to do (as he certainly could)! There's such a thing as freedom of choice in Britain, he told, them, and 'I don't choose to speak or write as you choose to do, so bugger of and mind your own business.'

As a result of which, Robert did not socialise or hang out with most of these working-class neighbours and their bully-boy children, but kept company with middle and upper class people instead, none of whom lived where he lived or went to school where he went to school; but virtually all of whom were very pleased to know him (especially the girls and young women, many of whom he dated). He did this by frequenting middle and upper class meeting places and hangouts and getting to know a different social set that welcomed him and gave him a leg up whenever possible (as well as a leg over before long in his late teens!).

Being utterly against the foolishness and madness of the class system and its class war, there was nothing snooty or defensive about Robert; he was, rather, practical rather than snooty, as he spoke as he found people, and by and large he found middle and upper class people very congenial and broad-minded and no better or worse ethically or morally than their less broad minded working-class 'inferiors' who regularly rubbished the middle and upper classes because they were culturally and socially prejudiced against their so-called 'superior' ways.

Robert had none of these chips on his shoulder and wanted none of this inferior/superior hullabaloo – he just wanted to speak and write English correctly as it was best spoken and to be left alone to do his own thing. If others wanted to speak and write it poorly or badly, let them get on with it, but count him out!

But in the 1950s, he was up against almost some 1,500 years of regionally and badly spoken and written English since the time of the first Anglo-Saxon settlers in England from Germany, way before the gradual and slow beginnings of standardised and 'received' English in the 1800s – no that he or the kids in his neighbourhood or school had any idea of this – which was when the country was riddled with the different dialects and accents from different tribes in so many different regions whose local language was comprehensible only or largely to those that lived there rather than outsiders against whom they were prejudiced because they did not know or trust them, or wish to know or trust them, and against whom they asserted their local/regional identify by reason of their accents, closing ranks with those that spoke like them, but against others that did not do so or refused to do so!

All crazy and ignorant thinking and speaking!

Not until 1836 - a staggering 186 years ago – did standardised and correctly spoken and written English get into the English Dictionary as officially 'received' English.

One can well imagine the tiny and closed highly-prejudiced and very primitive minds that went with these different regional languages among backward and very insular people in Britain who never travelled outside their community to meet with and converse with others in the same country or perhaps even the same county!

And it wasn't only the ordinary people who had, or had had, all these differently closed languages and minds (the two were made for each other) – had them respectively in different parts of the same country - but many if not most of their leaders and even some of their monarchs as well for the greater part of this 1500-year history; all unbelievably true!

There were even occasional monarchs from abroad who spoke no English at all, *mein gott.*

In view of this 1500-year-old or thereabouts anthropology with its regional-language prejudices and psycho dynamics in the very air that a lot of people still breathed for centuries (without their realising it necessarily), it is and was hardly surprising that a 20th-century child with half a brain at least in the 1950s, might want none of it (even so, a great many still did prefer to cling to it in this human zoo, not having the confidence to give well-spoken English a try!) – it is hardly surprising that such a child as Robert did not want to say 'them people,' for example, rather than 'those people,' and refused to do so. Yet most of the children that ganged up on Robert were not merely surprised, but ignorantly outraged by his superior English that they seriously resented!

Robert told them: 'Not only do you eat junk food, you speak and talk junk English as well.'

Many of these rubbish accents and dialects in different parts of Britain had been so thick and incomprehensible and meaningless to others from other regions, that it is a wonder that it took such a long time for people to see the error of their stupid ways and to eventually standardise their English into one mutually comprehensible spoken and written tongue with its necessary and long-overdue grammatical rules and agreed spellings (and never mind the occasional contradictions) for the greater clarification of one and all; all of which Robert was keen and determined to learn regardless of his working-class origins, while most of his neighbours and their children were not at all keen or determined. For all they cared, others would just have to live with their mispronunciations, bad spellings and bad grammar, given that these others could still understand what they were saying, since their latest local accents were no longer 1,500 years old and thick and crusty-rusty (they had become marginally less crusty and rusty over the centuries).

In the fullness of time – when Robert became an adult – most of his friends and contacts automatically assumed from his naturally relaxed and unaffected speaking voice – that was in no way exaggerated or snooty – that he was middle or upper-middle class, as indeed he was, by reason of his employment, income and where he lived at the higher end of the social ladder.

Readers who think that all this stuff about problematic regional accents is or may be exaggerated, are invited to take the following little test to see if they can understand

England's longest-surviving regional dialect and thickest accent from Geordie Land – Newcastle and the North East – and see how many of the answers they get wrong or simply do not know.

What is the meaning of: gannin; yem; clammin; howay; canny; way aye; what ye uptee the neet; I divvina; gizza deek; in a fettle; haddaway.

Whilst the local spoken and written 'country' accents where Robert lived and went to school in the Southeast, were nowhere near as incomprehensible as this, they were to a lesser extent all part of the same social, educational and class problem when it came to getting language right rather than wrong.

Jacko Jackson had finished up as head master of Robert's working-class school, after World War Two when many an 'officer class' person went down market in order to get a decent job, and given that he was brilliant at maths, he was by far the best candidate (given also that he knew how to command what needed to be commanded).

The chances are that he was the best maths teacher and head master to be found in such a school or community and Robert felt that the school was lucky to have him. There was nothing politically or sociologically ideological about him, he just believed in education for its own sake, as well as in doing a job properly as and when it was worth doing. He did not want to change the world or society and make it a better place, but he did want to prevent it from becoming any worse.

With a large skull and receding black hair, dark eyes and a square and jutting jaw that was very pronounced, he was an upright, fine figure of a man, with a back as straight as a ram-rod, and he had seen military action during World War Two. Because he did not usually invite boys into his study unless to reprimand them for something, or maybe to cane them, Robert was wondering what he might have done wrong!

There were all sorts of misdeeds for punishing and/or caning boys in the school's punishment book – a book that was generally to be found in all such schools in the UK and not just his school – and they included repeatedly careless work and regularly talking in class, seriously troublesome behaviour, regular late arrival at school, or truancy from school, stealing and aggressive behaviour, riding bicycles on pavements or in the school playground, consistently running along school corridors or up and down stairs, shouting, being repeatedly scruffy, dirty and unwashed, spitting in school, using airguns, catapults and other weapons, regularly telling lies, disrespecting teachers and disobeying them, disrupting classes and bullying other children.

Many children were entirely capable of all these things, but they were not capable of getting away with them with Jacko Jackson. So there was as much caning going on in the school as teaching and learning!

Bedlam!

New boys were welcomed and broken in by older boys when they first arrived at the junior school by stuffing the juniors into waste bins and rolling them round the playground – no wheelie bins in those days – and this was another thing that Robert flatly refused to be subject do, putting up such a fist fight that his persecutors thought better of it and left him alone!

Whilst Robert was not a naturally violent child, he could stand up to and overcome violence on a needs-must basis.

But one of his closest friends – called David Collis - could not, alas, and had a nervous breakdown as a result of this barbarism, he who eventually finished up doing a French and German Language degree at university, before switching to Psychology and finishing up as a school teacher in the private fee-paying sector.

Boys could be punished with the cane on their bottoms, or a ruler on their fingers, whilst both boys and girls were kept in after school for as long as one hour to write out dozens or hundreds of lines, repeating line after line that they must not do this or that or something else.

A strapping great fellow, over six feet tall, with broad shoulders, Jackson could handle himself in the boxing ring, and he could certainly handle the roughest and toughest of the working-class fathers who had their children in his well-classified and describe 'secondary old' school for state school children who lived in the mean streets in the immediate vicinity of this so-called place of learning that was very secondary and very old and behind the times in so many ways.

Jacko frequently sparred with his physical training teacher – a former marine commando - in the school boxing ring and, on parent's evenings, he organised for the entertainment of his pupils, their mothers and his female staff, very popular rough and ready knockabout games in the school gym for fathers and male staff (probably he was sending a message!).

These games included good-humoured wrestling for any father that fancied his chances against him, adult pillow-fights and a version of pass the parcel that included wrestling in order to hang on to the parcel once it had been passed to you. It wasn't enough to be in possession of the parcel when the music stopped, you had to prevent the men sitting on either side of you in the circle of contestants from wrestling it out of your hands. They were allowed five minutes to wrestle it out of your hands if they could.

This really was a shock-horror school in more ways than one, a school from hell for sensitive children (Robert was not that sensitive, but many were, whilst Robert was permanently discomforted).

When rough and tough, quarrelsome working-class fathers waited outside the school gates to pick on teachers who had got on the wrong side of their rowdy and unruly children, as they so often did, Jacko was down at the gates like a bullet out of a gun to see these fathers off, as he never failed to do, challenging them to fisticuffs in the school boxing ring if they cared to take him on, as they never did.

School bullies who picked on weaker children in the playground were ordered into the boxing ring with bigger boys who were more than a match for these bullies and pleased to welcome them as sparring partner punch-bags because they were regularly in training for the school's boxing team that fought against other schools.

Few of these bullies wanted to go into the ring with boys who could outbox them, so they could choose between Jacko's cane and a champion schoolboy boxer. Tiresome others who became a nuisance in the playground, because they repeatedly fought each other there when they were told not to by teachers, were sent into the ring to finally resolve their differences under the watchful eye of the physical training instructor who refereed them.

This is how Jacko ran his 1940s and 1950s school and with the full approval, of the local education authority and parents, given that neither tabled any formal complaints against him, probably because he had a well-deserved reputation of being, not only a hard man, but also a fair man, a fair but firm man. Few of the parents at the school kidded themselves that their children were angels and they expected school teachers to discipline their children for them, as firmly as they disciplined these children themselves in their homes (many fathers kept canes in their houses – hanging on living room walls – or otherwise took their belts off to their sons to strap them when they were out of order).

As we see from all this, the past is indeed not just another country, but sometimes another planet!

Which is why this school was such a culture shock for Roberts's aforesaid friend, David - who lived a couple of streets away from him - that he had his nervous breakdown and was transferred from his shocking school to another in a more genteel neighbourhood, and his transfer from this school school from hell turned out to be a blessing in disguise, because the other more genteel and better school to which he went, gave him a much better education that eventually got him into university, via the local Grammar. In future years he would joke that his superior education started inside a waste bin!

Whenever Jacko caned boys, he did not just tap them on their bottoms in a perfunctory way, but instructed them to bend over at the far end of the long room that served as his study, so that he could run at them from the other end in order to gather speed for maximum impact by the time that his cane struck them with a mighty whack!

But he was otherwise kindly and caring, he really was, with a son of his own who was destined to follow in his father's footsteps and become a school teacher and ultimately a headmaster in due course.

Coming from lowly circumstances and a humble home, Robert, by contrast, was theoretically and supposedly destined to follow in his father's footsteps and become 'a plasterer like his dad,' as his mother liked to put it, labouring on building sites. But Robert had very different ideas about this and, as we shall see in this story, he had no intention of becoming a plasterer. On the contrary, he was an extraordinary boy who intended to get himself educated and to find a professional white-collar job, notwithstanding the social and educational handicaps for working-class children back then. He had every intention of taking his destiny and/or fate into his own hands and changing it for himself. He was by far the brightest pupil in his year and was being prepared in consequence for transfer to a nearby grammar school that had agreed, in principle, to take him.

Whilst he was obviously no genius (as some children are), his IQ was firing on all cylinders and who was to say what he may become for the better, given a decent educational chance?

His father told him: 'Well done, Robert, don't become a plasterer or building worker like me, whatever you do. Don't listen to your mother.'

But his mother wanted him out of school and working in order to bring in the urgently needed pennies and pounds that kept the wolf from the family door.

She, like most other working-class women in the street where she and her family lived, was such a hard-working woman that she had no idea of a better life 'for her kind,' as she also liked to put it, without working right round the clock. She could not – would not – imagine it otherwise, not for her class of person. What else was there, and what need for higher education was there, therefore? Her kind did the menial jobs that the middle and upper classes had no interest in doing and seldom, if at all, did any of the working classes get into the professions, not that she could see. Her kind knew their place, had their place, and there was nothing to be done about it, other than getting on with it.

It was a life, not only of people knowing their place and deferring to their royals far too much in those days, but of taking pride in their place and being reasonably content with it and also their deferment; rather than ashamed of it, which was wrong in principle, of course, but in reality socially right in practise in the opinion of Robert's mother and her parents, where their much-needed pride and the contentment was concerned, how could they be expected to live without at least a ration of pride and contentment to keep them going (self-worth and self-belief!), rather than taking to the streets and trashing the place with a bloody revolution (as had happened in other countries where royal and other heads had rolled). If salt was rubbed into their working-class wounds by denying them pride and contentment at their lowly level – adding insult to their injury thereby – where would that leave them psychologically and emotionally?

Don't all answer at once!

Robert was absolutely against rubbing salt into working-class or any other kind of wounds and frequently said so, which is why he did not favour a class war (or any other kind of war for that matter, unless it absolutely could not be avoided) in order to solve the problem.

He stood for a much more intelligent solution and did not believe that war and/or revolution was the only option.

All this and more was regularly discussed and debated in his and other working-class homes that were – in his retrospective view much later in his life - much more politically literate in the 1950s than they had been previously and also became subsequently.

These homes represented the unenviable reality of the history that the working-classes had inherited – that they had been lumbered if not clobbered with – the reality of how they made the most and the best of it or the worst of it, with a pecking order in which each and every person, family and social sector was expected to know its place, be content with it and modestly proud of it, deferring to others above them on the social ladder with the royals at the top of the totem pole, unifying them all and keeping them all reasonably respectful to one another and not least to their betters!

With common consent, this was better by far than a bloody revolution in favour of communism, republicanism or fascism, as had happened in Continental European countries, such as Russia, France and Germany, for instance, and these were the beliefs and conventions with which most Brits were brought up, thinking themselves better than other races in this notable respect.

Robert's father chuckled, as he observed that the British working classes – several of whom worked for him (a small businessman) in order to put bread on their tables – had learned how to be grateful for small mercies, rather than upsetting the social and political applecart big time and making matters as lot worse!

He argued that the greatest gift to the British establishment and keeping it in tact was the existence of Communism or Fascism, both of which were anathema and distasteful to the British working and other classes, which is why they would not upset the applecart in its favour – on the contrary they would all close their ranks against it, with the working-classes settling for a lesser life that they did not believe would be improved by communism or fascism.

The working-classes were generally content with and had settled for cheap beer, cheap tobacco and cigarettes, low rents for terrace houses and council flats they could never afford to buy and did not want to buy, content as they were with an affordable cheap 1950s bargain-basement life in which prices were kept low for the likes of them, while the trade unions shouted loudly for reform but got nowhere fast much if not most of the time, thanks to the cloth ears of their audience!

Of course they had (and had had) their industrial unrest and wildcat strikes, but never significantly more than that, and those that were lucky enough to work for Robert's father (not more than a dozen for much of the time) were paid well above the minimum wage whenever he could afford it, as he often could; for this reason, he had no time or need for trade unions and would not join their political movement, or tolerate any interference from them, which of course made him very unpopular with their leaders and shop stewards, not that he cared what they thought of him, he who was his own man and a very fair-minded employer who always treated his men and their families decently and with concern, so he wanted nothing whatsoever to do with the group-think or politicking of the unions – with their 'we'll tell you what to do think' – that had too many 'bigoted macho-idiots' in his opinion, too many 'personality conflicts' and

'internal power struggles.'

In the absence of adequate social benefits (that he regarded a disgrace), he once made the financial sacrifice to pay his brother an income and to provide for his family for a whole year after a motorbike accident had disabled him, taking Robert to visit him and his family in his council house, not that his brother had ever been an employee of his!

This was the kind of very decent man that he was and why Robert respected him so much, for doing the decent thing whenever he could, and even when he could not, when he made the necessary sacrifices to *find a way* of doing the decent thing.

As we see, Robert was brought up with the very best of ethical and moral influences, not that they were ever preached out loud in his home where they were observed and learned much more by example than by didactic teaching.

All this – and more yet - was the established order of things and how they were operating, as Robert knew and understood them, from a very young age, with Queen and Country to the fore of that order and figure-heading it, and most else all part of a social contract that followed from it.

But before long – within ten and twenty years, back in the 1950s, the new Queen Elizabeth II and her husband started to chip and kick against this obsolete order with its convention of deferment to the mystique of British royals and their very firmly established order, chipping and kicking from inside the British establishment and paving the way for future generations of much more socially and intelligently liberated and grown-up people – among royalists and their fans equally at all levels of society – and they did so by deliberately destroying their mystique by letting the television cameras into their personal lives, televising their royal coronation for all – for starters - to see for the first time in history (absolutely against the advice of their advisors and prime minister Winston Churchill), while also consenting to a fly-on-the-wall reality TV show about them at home.

In this way they started to reach out to their people and get rid of the traditional deferment of the generation of Robert's parents and grandparents, getting closer to and becoming more popular with people in this way (and when their royal children and grandchildren grew up in later years, some of them did likewise and with much more constitutional outspokenness).

Predictably this was a very topical if not controversial matter back in the 1950s in working-class, middle-class and upper-class homes – apart from those that remained tight-lipped about these matters because they were afflicted with such a peculiar and incurable condition! – and it was a matter that was a regular topic of discussion and debate in Robert's home where his mother was against more populist familiarity with royals, whilst his father was in favour, up to a reasonable point (as in all things, reasonable man that he was!). But his mother wanted her royals set apart from the common herd and respected from afar.

She and her husband were right-wing conservatives – she for ideological and almost religious and worshipful reasons! – but he for practical reasons to do with the workplace and keeping the interfering and bullying trade unions out of his affairs.

She was a very practical woman married to a very practical man and we shall come to her later in this story, but suffice it to say for the time being that her long day began at the crack and smack of dawn when she lit the coal fires that kept her family home warm from the kitchen (called scullery), to the living room and also the front room bedsit where she looked after her retired father in his dotage.

She looked after him, in addition to everybody else in her five-member family, and she knew nothing of such mod cons as easily switched on and off electric fires that were unheard of to her, or of the science fiction of turning a simple switch or pressing a button to activate the central heating that keeps houses warm today.

So lighting these fires was, in itself, a demanding task, putting heavy lumps of coal into a bucket and carrying them from the coal shed to the coal fires, as soon as she fell out of bed every morning in her cold house other than summer time that was hardly ever hot. But at least she and her family knew nothing of fuel poverty, because the coal was cheap and plentiful enough. The fire in her kitchen had to be lit under the oven, before she could boil a kettle of water on a hot plate above it and make herself her first cup and pot of tea for the day, and before she could make breakfast for her husband and children, the former of whom was also up at the crack and smack of dawn and on his way to the building sites where he toiled long and hard as a plasterer, supervising the men that he employed (half a dozen or a dozen, depending on how much business he had).

She progressed from the kitchen to her adjacent living room to light her second fire – a time-consuming process, not without risk, because after she had cleaned out the ashes in the grate under her living room fire – ashes from the night before - she had to break up pieces of splintered wood and get them to kindle with loosely screwed-up balls of newspaper, so that the coal would eventually burn when she put it into the flames from the kindle. In order to accelerate this tricky process, she stretched out both her arms wide, to hold up a double-page spread of newspaper over the front of the open fire, like a screen, so that a vacuum could be created on the other side and inside of the paper, and trap what was left of the air there, so that it shot up the chimney with the flames and sucked and sped the latter with it.

The skill or practised art was to hold the double-page spread of newspaper carefully in place without its being caught by the flames in the smouldering paper between her hands and in her face! So the paper had to be held not too close and not too far from the flames if it was not to go up in flames. Once she had lit the living room fire in this precarious way, she then moved on to the third and final fire in her front room bedsit before making breakfast for her father there, after she had made it for her husband also, in the living room.

But this was only the beginning of all her other arduous and tedious, scrubbing and cleaning, sweeping and dusting, clothes washing and clothes mangling/drying, physical tasks in a house completely bereft of any labour-saving devices or mod cons, bereft of modern washing machines, dryers, dishwashers and the like, each and all of which we shall come to before we are through with this story.

As for Robert, she got him and his brothers out of bed and off to school in the morning by opening all the bedroom windows and letting the cold air into the house upstairs, before stripping the blankets from her children's beds, so that they would jump out of bed and get dressed fast and rush down stairs in time for breakfast and be warmed by the open fires there!

And as for Princess Elizabeth when she became Queen of England, well she was the only female icon that mattered to Robert's mother, this fairy-tale woman in her palace, running the country and telling all the men what to do and making sure that they treated her nicely!

Which woman wouldn't want to be treated nicely by men and have them grovelling at her feet and treating her nicely as they obeyed her every command?

Queen Elizabeth had it made!

How Robert's mother approved of Queen Elizabeth II – a woman in charge at last!

Robert was in no way apprehensive or scared of headmaster Jacko Jackson on account of his cane, as he made his way to his office, having been mysteriously summoned there. This was because this head master was no bully and also because caning wilfully disruptive or disobedient schoolboys was no big deal in those distant times (the 1950s and before). It was nothing to fret or complain about because it was considered normal and was generally accepted that schoolboys needed to be disciplined in this way. Given that, as happened, Robert liked and respected this headmaster, who did a good job in his view, with so many disobedient and unruly children on his hands who, to tell the truth, were not interested to get themselves educated, and who objected to others that were, disrupting their classes if they could get away with it.

'Take a seat, Robert, I have something to tell you.'

'Thank you, sir.'

'To mark the Coronation of Queen Elizabeth II this year, a royal prize is being offered next year to the most public spirited and able schoolchild in this school. The prize will be inscribed with the words The 1954 Queen Elizabeth II Coronation Prize and it will go to the child with the best combined record of academic, sporting and community work.'

'Really, sir? How interesting.'

'I am glad you think so, Robert, because I have discussed the matter with the teaching staff and we are all unanimously agreed that you and two other children should be nominated for this prize for the most outstanding pupil. Only one of you will win it, but we believe that we have three children who are worthy of consideration. I am speaking to each child individually to put them on notice and I am yet to speak to the other two. It will take a little while for each teacher to individually study the respective records of the three best children and then cast his or her vote in favour of one of them, but the process has already begun, and there are not more than three outstanding contestants that we can seriously put forward, so it shouldn't take too long to get all the votes in from teachers.'

'I see, sir.'

'But then it will take a while longer for the local council and education authority to issue the prize. Not just this prize, but others besides for other schools, and not just prizes for schools, but also souvenir medals, spoons, drinking glasses, pens and the like for all children, so that every child gets something – not a prize but some memorabilia, which it looks as though the education authority will be supplying as well. For this reason, we may have to wait until early next year or later this before these prizes are awarded and the all memorabilia is distributed, not that next year is far off now, given that we are fast approaching the end of this year.'

A Coronation Celebration Committee had been set up by the local council in the previous year. This was a committee consisting of the bishop of the town, the vice-chancellor of the local university, the presidents of the local chambers of commerce and trade, as well as the editors of two local newspapers. This committee reported in turn to the town council's education and finance committees, not that Robert had the slightest clue about any of this.

Jacko Jackson went on to explain: 'Prizes are being awarded to children in other schools in this town and throughout the county and country, if enough schools can be found to come forward with suitably outstanding pupils that they can confidently recommend. Not all can, but many can. Some schools are having essay writing competitions on the subject of royalty and our new Queen, but this school is looking for actions not words - so no essay writing competition here. Schools with pupils incapable of prizes will have to settle for souvenir memorabilia instead of prizes. But for a winner of the prize for which you are being nominated, Robert, this school is setting its own criteria and looking for pupils who are as good on the sports field as they are in the class room and also in the local community where children have distinguished themselves in some way. The word is that this is what Queen Elizabeth II prefers, but neither the local education authority nor the local council are interested to set the criteria for a coronation prize of this kind for the most outstanding child in the town - which is a big mistake in my view – so different schools are awarding different prizes for different reasons. But this school is awarding the prize for the best all-rounder. So there are not too many in this school that can be recommended for such a prize, but you are definitely one of them.'

'Crikey!'

'Crikey, indeed. Not bad for a fourteen-year-old like you, Robert, to be nominated for such a prize, and all the more impressive if you should win it. At this level of schooling, one can be of any age, from eleven to fifteen or sixteen years of age, few stay on after fifteen. Probably the prize will be judged and awarded differently by different education authorities in different parts and regions of the country where standards vary. But this is how it will be awarded here.'

'Will the winner get to meet the Queen?'

'Good god! Don't be ridiculous, Robert, of course not. She won't have time for that. She only meets the great and the good. Whichever children win her prizes will remain completely unknown to her. But that's alright. Nothing at all unusual about that. You cannot expect monarchs to go and meet unknown school children just because they have won some prizes, not in this day and age.'

It was a suddenly puzzled and pensive schoolboy who replied, 'oh, I see,' but not looking as though he saw any such thing (as he began to feel that he was rapidly losing his innocence!). He began to think that it couldn't be right that everybody knew and cared about a monarch that knew so little about them in return and presumably cared little also, otherwise such a monarch would make an effort to get to know their subjects better!

When Robert mentioned this to his father, he told his son that the chances were that these British monarchs knew more about foreigners than they did their own people! And probably the reason for this was, he suggested, that only by keeping their own people in the dark about them, could monarchs keep their people in place – too much familiarity would breed contempt, perhaps, so mystique was reckoned to be essential for the survival of monarchy, and indeed the social order and racial unity of the nation. Robert's father explained that he wasn't knocking it – or seeking to rock the boat and make waves – but simply explaining it and how he perceived that it worked.

In other words, the ordinary people were being socially engineered in a politically calculated way – massively calculated – to keep them loyal to their monarchy by using mystique about it to cast its spell upon them that was not unlike the spell of religion, with which it was exercised, hand in glove, and in the name of God.

For as long as the ordinary people fell for the mystique of religion or monarchy, then all would be well (or might otherwise be worse!)

Robert's father reckoned that this was the theory in which a great many of the people believed, or were expected to believe, but it seemed to young Robert that it was in fact a gigantic con, and when he suggested this to his father, he told Robert: 'Don't tell your mother that, whatever you do! She will clip your ear in no time at all, if you do. There's a widespread, tribal belief in this country, that monarchs are needed to keep us all in good order for the good of the tribe, with a monarch at the head of the national totem pole, so it would be nothing less than heresy to go against the ancient grain and mindset of this belief in the fantasy of monarchy.'

'What's a heresy?' Robert wanted to know.

'A disbelief in an all-powerful God or leader.'

'You mean a monarch as God here on earth rather than a God in heaven?'

'That's' right and for nationalist and tribal rather than spiritual reasons. It's a blasphemy, of course, but a good rather than a bad blasphemy, and much better than the blasphemy that comes with a communist or fascist tin-god leader, for example.'

'And what's a fantasy.'

'Make believe. When you pretend that something is true because you want it to be so for whatever reason. When you imagine it to be true and you imagine it for long enough and strongly enough that it actually becomes kind of true, at least in your imagination, if not in reality and the harsh light of day.'

'Do you believe in monarchy, dad?'

'Not really, not for me personally. But I do believe that it's a harmless fantasy that works well for a lot of people – like religion itself – and if that's what tribal people need to keep them on track psychologically and emotionally, then there's no harm in it maybe, as long as it does keep them on track within reasonable limits, as it seems to do for most people in this country, otherwise they would have had a revolution and become republicans like the French and others before them who have got rid of their monarchies. It certainly works for your mother and a goodly number of other women like her in this country and now that they are getting a female goddess in the form of Princess Elizabeth, the new Queen Elizabeth II, they are over the moon! So let them be over the moon once in a while, where's the harm in their humdrum lives?'

Of course, 1954 was to be more memorable for other things than simply for the year in which Robert's school awarded its Queen Elizabeth II Coronation prize.

Wartime food rationing did not come to an end until 1954, nine years after the close of World War Two. So Britain really was a very different place in those days, difficult to imagine if one did not live through those hard times - difficult to get the feel and the atmosphere of the place.

World War Two, from 1939 to 1945, had lasted some six years, but the disastrous
after effects continued long afterwards.

There was no passenger air terminal at London's Heathrow Airport in 1954 – that came the following year when it was officially opened by Queen Elizabeth II – and fourteen-year-old Robert was in the habit of arduously pedal cycling to Heathrow some thirty-two miles from his home-town to see what was going on. He cycled there on a bicycle that he had purchased with moneys saved from a daily newspaper round, going from house to house putting newspapers through letter boxes early each morning before going to school, and then again in the evenings after he returned from school, and he had got it into his head from delivering different newspapers that it might be a rather interesting life to be a journalist when he grew up.

The medical student Roger Bannister broke the four-minute mile up at Oxford University in 1954 and Robert cheered him on over the radio, because the event was not televised. Like Robert, Roger Bannister came from lowly social circumstances and state schools, and was destined to become a doctor and professor of medicine.

The world's first passenger jet – the Boeing 707 out of the United States – made its debut flight in 1954, the same year that the United States put its first nuclear weapons base for cruise missiles into Britain, at Greenham Common, to deter possible communist attacks from an ever-threatening Soviet Union. This potentially explosive base was a dozen miles or so from where Robert lived and went to school. It was where, later on, he would play football for a local amateur football club near to the base (Padworth Football Club). The United States launched its first atomic submarine – the *US Nautilus* – during 1954 whilst at the same time testing a nuclear bomb that was 1,000 times more powerful and destructive than the one dropped on Hiroshima in Japan during World War Two.

There was a siege mentality in Britain and Europe in 1954, with much uncertainty and doom and gloom for a child to take in – as there had been in 1939 when Robert had been born on Sept 11 at the outbreak of World War Two – and 1954 was also the year when there was a peace pact between warring communist China and democratic India (whilst, in the United States, the world's first shopping mall was opened, in Michigan, and the US Cancer Society announced that it 'suspected' that cigarette smoking may contribute to lung cancer!).

It was in this all-happening and ominously threatening political and military climate, with its heavily uncertain and not exactly cloudless atmosphere, that young Robert was being nominated for a sunny little Queen Elizabeth II Coronation Prize on this singularly joyous occasion.

Whilst there were other pupils in the school who were more popular with their teachers than Robert, these pupils were not such outstanding all-rounders as he, so he was far from being an unpopular candidate with the teaching staff, added to which he was a house captain.

Probably he was not sufficient of a teacher's pet and was too independently minded for some members of staff, and perhaps he tended to know his own mind and go his own way more than they would have wished, but he was by no means out of favour on account of being his own man. So, all things considered, he was popular enough for them all to honestly agree that he was worthy of being put forward for this prize, if not to win it on the strength of his record of achievements.

Because this was a time in British history when familiarity between school teachers and their pupils was not encouraged, relations and conversations between them were more formal and restrained than they are today and not in any way chatty, yet here was Robert having a 'chat' with the head, albeit not exactly an informal or chatty chat, but a chat for all that. For the most part, the head was doing all the talking and

Robert was listening (waiting patiently for the right moment to get a word in here and there!).

The head master explained that: 'In order to qualify for the prize, a child has to perform well outside the school in the local community, as well as inside the school in the classroom. But the final emphasis is on public spiritedness. In addition to being a good and able pupil in the classroom, a child must also distinguish itself on the sports field and in the community. It's the best all-rounder who will win this prize.'

The word was that the prize was the wish of the former Princess Elizabeth who had become Queen Elizabeth II following the death of her father George V1 in 1952 and after marrying Prince Philip in 1947 - a couple of years after the end of World War Two in 1945 - when spirits needed to be massively lifted for several years to come in Britain, which was a very austere and gloomy place in those post-war years for almost a decade afterwards, and not least in 1953 when Elizabeth's coronation took place.

Britain had been and still was in the doldrums during the war's aftermath when food rationing continued and times were still very hard for the vast majority of people, as they were for Robert and his parents. By the end of the war it was reported that some 92,673 civilians and 264, 443 combatants (including 35,000 merchant seamen) had been killed from the UK, and predictably this cast a long shadow over British communities.

These were communities in which many thousands had been injured and killed in bombing raids at home, as well as thousand more that had been injured on the battlefields abroad. There was desolation, destruction and bomb damage to be seen without people having to look very far to find it and many parts of the UK were wastelands. But many more people had been killed in other countries than in Britain – especially in Soviet Russia (a staggering 11 million combatants and 7 million civilians) and Germany (3.5 million combatants and 780,000 civilians) – but enough had been killed in Britain to make the point that war is a mugs' game, not that this ever seemed to deter countries from going to war!

Then, of course, some 5.7 million Jews had sadly-badly and disgracefully died or been put to death in Nazi concentration camps, and not least Polish Jews (3.2 million), whilst the Japanese had lost 1.3 million combatants and 672,000 civilians. Whilst Robert and his parents and others like them were not aware of these precise figures at the time, they became gradually aware of them in the slow fullness of time, as they read books about the ugly spectre of war in which these figures sometimes varied, but not by very much, and also as they acquired encyclopaedia books in years to come (in Robert's case a *Macmillan Encyclopaedia* for a final death count) when the dust finally settled and the truly dreadful figures finally clarified to the horror of one and all. War story films and newsreel films also spread the details of the full horrors of World War Two, all of which was the cultural wallpaper of the time.

As we have seen in this chapter, these were hard times that produced plenty of necessarily hard adults and children, hard school teachers and hard discipline, and also hard work and hard wars. In Robert's opinion they were also hard-luck times for the hardship people that had no choice but to survive these years of toil and struggle, people who wished for better, softer and more civilising and peaceful times, which is of course why the 1960s were welcomed with open arms by the vast majority of people in Britain's new-look society that suddenly emerged without too much warning, described by prime minister Harold Macmillan as 'you've never had it so good' times (merely because more modern homes were suddenly and gradually being built and also because these times could not have been more bad than they were previously, strange logic for the word 'good!').

When the war was over and the fleetingly joyous and victorious street parties came to an end – with all their colourful bunting, balloons, cupcakes, lemonade and ginger beer – happiness and relief sank swiftly like a lead balloon, because life was no party, and there wasn't much left to be joyous or celebratory about in a threadbare down-at-heel country greatly impoverished by the conflict and stricken with the rubble of bomb damage that took a long time to clear. Children grew up with all this, much of which remained ingrained in their tender memories. These were dim and dismal, lasting memories, to interpret and to learn to live with as best they could or could not. Precious memories of un-precious times! Memories about a bitter-sweet life that had been, alas, anything but precious, and about ragged post-war working-class children who grew up with rickets, ring-worms, whooping cough and tuberculosis, and precious few social and educational prospects for self-improvement.

It was estimated that it had cost Britain some £10 million a day to defend itself against Hitler's Germany and when in 1952 the young Elizabeth became Queen, at the age of 25 years, she reigned over a kingdom in which 4.5 million people had no bath tubs in their homes, 900,000 were without a toilet and 690,000 had no water.

Whilst the new young Queen had her head and shoulders printed on British postal stamps, there were few in the British working classes who used these stamps very often, either because they had nobody to write to on a regular basis, or because they were counting their pennies and shillings and had better things to do with their money! These were the days when a precious penny went quite a long way. Children could get a penny's worth or farthing's worth of sweets back then, not that their parents had too many pennies to give them. A farthing was one quarter of a penny and there was in Yorkshire a Penny Bank that encouraged people to save their pennies for a rainy day. By contrast, the new Queen of England inherited millions if not billions of pounds and had more gold and precious jewels than she knew what to do with when she was the richest woman on the planet back then!

The snail's pace of recovery after World War Two was slow indeed and had to be seen to be believed. Many of the aforesaid run-down homes had been in a miserably poor condition even before the war began!

With more than 2 million people unemployed and those in work toiling for long hours in return for very small incomes – and no social security - there was chronic economic depression and plenty of misery in many places throughout Elizabeth's kingdom, as people stretched themselves to make a little go a long way. Making a little go a long way was what they were good at.

The word was that, when Adolph Hitler came to power in 1930s Nazi Germany – in order to keep the communists out of power in that country – there had been 3 million Germans unemployed, hungry, angry and on the march!

To make matters worse in the 1950s, a Third World War was usually expected to be waged against the Communist East (principally Russian and China) with atomic weapons that would finally destroy the entire world, once and for all, bringing about the end of all human life as we know it.

A post-war generation grew up in a spine-chilling atmosphere of increasingly uneasy calm that was, predictably, far from easy on the nerves, as children came along in the painful knowledge all this. The ominous thought of being invaded by Communist Russia so soon after a narrowly failed attempt at invasion by Hitler's Germany was not exactly music to a child's ears! As a result, children's spirits and the spirits of their parents were thought to be in need of a lift,

58

which is why they packed into their local cinemas at least once, or maybe even twice a week, to watch cheaply priced movies that got their minds off the dim and grim reality of their everyday lives – in cheap and affordable cinemas nicknamed 'the flicks.'

They were nicknamed the flicks because it was there that the images of cowboys and Indians, comedians, criminals, romantic heroes and heroines, as well as, for good measure, images from triumphant and victorious war films, all flicked and flickered across the cinema screens, together with newsreels once a week in the absence of television in the homes of the vast majority of people.

Children's parents and grandparents had graduated from the silent movies of the 1900s to the sound-cinema movies of the late 1920s, thirties and forties when the so-called Golden Age of Hollywood Films (1930 to 1945) - that great entertainments factory of the world - had been at its height in the United States, increasingly over-spilling into Britain after the Second World War.

But it had been – not that anybody realised it - the French, not the Americans, who invented films in 1895 (the Lumiere brothers) and Robert did not realise this either, not until much later on in his adult life when he would have reason to visit the Lumiere brother's museum and birthplace in France to learn about this.

Every Friday night was film night for Robert and his parents and their neighbours, because Friday was 'pay day,' when husbands were paid their very modest weekly wages and could just about afford to take their families to the flicks, and how they all looked forward to that. And the following Saturday morning was 'children's cinema' at half the price of Friday night, to which all kids generally went once again, so that their parents could get them off their hands, just as the following Sunday morning the same children went to 'Sunday school' at their local church for the same reason – so that their parents could get them off their hands.

This was the immediate background in British working-class communities up and down the country against which Queen Elizabeth II of England had come to her throne and held her coronation, with prizes for school children to be issued in her name.

'I expect, Robert, you have seen in the daily newspapers how beautiful the young Queen Elizabeth is and you will also have seen her when you go to the movies and watch the newsreels'

'Yes, sir, she is a good looker, everybody says so.'

Within ten years of Elizabeth marrying while she was still a princess – between 1947 and 1957 - the Communist East really was expected to unleash atom bombs on the Capitalist West, wiping the tiny island of Britain off the face of the earth as soon as the war began, and two years before

Elizabeth became queen in 1952, North Korea (with China at its side) had invaded South Korea (with the United States at its side) in a military conflict that many feared had set the stage for a final showdown in the wider world between communism and capitalism. But twelve months later, during Elizabeth's coronation year in 1953, this war had ended indecisively, in a stalemate, until the next time perhaps, but not before 5 million had been killed.

As we see, Robert's generation of 'war babies' had been born with the strident and clashing music of war ringing in their ears. Not the soothing music of lullabies or other happy childhood songs and nursery rhymes, but the music of marching off to war.

During those early Cold War years – the term Cold War having been reportedly coined in 1947 by an American economic and political advisor to the US government called Bernard Baruch - it was widely assumed that the Korean War would escalate into a global conflict, which is why the British Socialist Prime Minister, Clement Attlee, had already committed his reasonably impoverished nation to re-arming at a cost of £3.4 million, which was a tenth of the national budget.

When Attlee came to power at the end of the war in 1945 – with a landslide victory over the war hero Winston Churchill who had been the previous prime minister during the war years (with Attlee as his deputy in a coalition government) – the newly popular Clement was committed to a socialist goal of full employment and greater social and educational equality for all (the conservative opposition had been committed to no such thing in its time), whilst at the same time, maintaining the nation's defences in the face of a new communist threat instead of a fascist Nazi threat as previously.

And Robert and his generation really did need greater social and educational equality, of which they had precious little!

The majority of Robert's working-class kind had to make do with limited (if not zero) educational opportunities of a very inferior kind. Only the few managed to get a decent education and Robert was determined to be one of them. He was determined to get into higher education by hook or by crook (he was like one of those kittens at the bottom of a pet-shop cage of cats that has to claw its way to the top because there are so many other cats above it!).

To make matters worse it was well understood in those distant days that all young children and adults would soon have to leave school and go off and perhaps fight yet another war when conscripted into the armed forces during their later teenage years, a war not against the despised Germans this time, but against despised others instead – Koreans, Russians maybe, Communists wherever they were to be found in the world (Malaysia, for example) and on an island colonised by the British in the Eastern Mediterranean Sea called Cyprus where the Greek and Turkish natives were daggers drawn.

Yet, people had had more than enough of tiresome war that never seemed to solve any of the problems for which the wars were supposedly being fought, other than the survival problem, hopefully, when one side suddenly moved against another.

People had had enough, at least in theory. They wanted to make peace, not war, if only a way could be found, as opposed to relying on the old belief that it takes a war to end a war.

There really was gloom and doom everywhere and, with good reason, because many if not most on planet earth really did seem think that the end of the world was very probably nigh, yet here was the headmaster of Robert's school cheerfully telling him that he was to be nominated for a prize from no less a person than the Queen of England.

The headmaster had some information about the prize printed in a leaflet that he asked Robert to read while he quickly left his study for a moment - to go and see one of his teachers about something or other - telling Robert that he would be back soon to hear what he thought about this prize for which he was being nominated with two other candidates, as a possible winner in 1954 - the year, let us not forget, that wartime rationing finally finished in Britain, having started in 1940 in the second year of World War Two.

To grasp the full psychological and emotional significance of rationing and all its memories eventually coming to an end in July 1954 – nine years after the finish of the Second World War – one needs to understand what exactly rationing was all about. It had been a government-controlled system that had been originally introduced to ration foodstuffs and clothes, only for the duration of the war. Having been introduced as a survival tactic when Hitler was trying to starve the British into submission – by sinking their merchant ships laden with imports – rationing had gone on and on for fourteen years, because Britain continued to be in short supply for almost another decade after the war!

During the war, British imports declined from 55 million tons of food per month to 12 million, which is why ration books were swiftly issued to all households that were restricted to a bare minimum of so many ounces or pounds of food per adult person per week or month, in exchange for cash and coupons out of their ration books, the latter of which stated their precise entitlement to their grocers and green grocers with whom these books had to be registered by every family in the country. There was no entitlement to buy without a coupon. Every time a purchase was made by a hungry customer, a coupon was cut out of a buff-coloured book for those without special needs - or otherwise crossed out and signed - by the grocers and greengrocers, so that it could not be used a second time.

Typically, each person was getting a weekly supply of not more than 2 ounces of butter, 8 of sugar, 2 of cheese, 1 fresh egg, 2 of tea, 4 of bacon, approximately a shilling's worth of meat (5/6p today), 4 of margarine, 2/3 pints of milk, 12 of sweets every four weeks, one packet of dried egg powder every 4 weeks, 1lb of jam every 2 months and so on. Another 16 points per month were allowed in order to enable customers some flexibility with which to pick and choose their own supplies. Fish, bread, rice, vegetables, canned fruit, cooking fat, cereals and biscuits were also subject to these tight restrictions, as were clothes, for which there were additional pink-coloured ration books limiting how many shirts, blouses, underclothes, handkerchiefs, socks, shoes, slippers, raincoats, trousers and skirts one could by with one's coupons.

Households were required to give details of the age and health of each person in their families in order to get these ration books, without which they really could not eat. Books were differently coloured – buff, pink, green and blue – for different purchases and also for different priorities for customers with different needs. For example, pregnant women and nursing mothers with children under five were issued with special-needs green books entitling them to marginally more rations than others in the supply of fruit, milk and eggs – more than one egg per week (depending on what was available), a daily pint of milk and first choice of available fruit. For growing children from five to sixteen years of age, there were special-needs blue books to ensure that they had first takings on meat in the event of worsening shortages and that they got half a pint of milk a day. The object of this tight control of strictly measured rations was to make sure that basic nutritional needs were regularly met and that everyone got roughly equal shares according to need in a rapidly dwindling food supply – to ensure that nobody went without or got less, while others got more, to ensure that there was no hoarding or price-hiking or black market.

But there was much cheating going on, especially in country districts where country folk had ready access from local farms and growers to more vegetables, eggs, butter and meat than people in the towns and cities. This was ready access to unofficial and illegitimate 'extra rations' that were sold on the side to the locals, additional to their legitimate rations, and they were also sold to grocers and green grocers in the towns and cities who sent lorries into the rural areas to purchase these supplies and profit from them. So there was a black market and not least in the posh hotels of the upper classes where more food was available at a price. There were also some employees whose employers provided free canteen and other meals, so they got more food than others by eating their employer's foods in the work place, whilst hoarding their ration-book foods at home. And then there were the American military bases in Britain that were oversupplied with foods - and also with nylon stockings for the British girlfriends of American airmen and soldiers - all of which found their way into local communities for the favoured few near to these bases, after the supplies had been flown in by American war 'planes that did not get sunk like the supply ships of the British Merchant Navy. There were also food parcels from well-wishers abroad - not least from Canada and South Africa - that were distributed by the British government to people's homes, as and when they arrived, one of the great delicacies of which was tinned sausages!

It was unbelievable that rationing lasted for fourteen years all the way through to 1954 long after the war- albeit with increasingly less severity - and then, when it suddenly came to an end, that too was unbelievable!

There was and there had been such a lot happening on so many different fronts for such a young lad as Robert, who was remembering and experiencing his life through flashbacks to his recent past – remembering was experiencing because without the latter (i.e. nothing to remember) there could be no former and vice-versa - whilst Robert's young mind also flashed forward to his 1954 present, with a ready consciousness that was forever with him, as he went over the same crazy ground, trying to make sense of it all; and although there were some flashbacks and flashes forward of which he could not make the clearest sense (or any whatsoever), there were other flashes that did make a lot of sense.

So he left the former to themselves and moved on to the latter. He was learning that without the clearest remembrance of the recent past in relation to his present, a complete and detailed consciousness of it all - with a bigger picture forever in the background of life's smaller picture - was not likely to develop (as we see, he was becoming a deep and serious thinker from quite a young age).

He had a talent for making the right connections between parallel and other events and developments in his life – rather than the wrong connections, as all too often happens, does it not? – and in this way he managed to piece together the most important things that were usefully shaping or badly misshaping and hindering his life and the person he wanted to be, with a view to getting rid of the latter. Rarely if at all did he compare apples with pears, or think that he was wrong when he was right, or right when he was wrong. His self-confidence and character was developing and strengthening fast in this way, as he had a very clear view of the kind of person he was and would settle for being, as opposed to being a reflection of dictatorial other children who attempted to reduce him to one of their herd, as – blindly – did his mother with her opposition to his receiving a grammar school and university education that she insisted that he did not need!

In order to hopefully outmanoeuvre his pesky mother and all these other pesky kids that were also educationally against him – as they threw their different spanners in his works – Robert was swiftly learning how to box clever (in other words diplomacy), as yet another string to his bow of teenage accomplishments (that would remain with him for decades afterwards). He was learning how to be diplomatic, up to a point, and then to be otherwise confrontational and unyielding beyond the point at which his diplomacy was failing.

The big thing that was badly mis-shaping his life and the person he never doubted that he was and was determined to be and/or become – when his bullying working-class peer group derided him for it and told him and threatened him that, with a standard BBC/Oxford English accent he was not allowed - was of course that this peer group that was so odious to him, was a persistently tiresome obstacle that he could do without, which is precisely what he did, he did without it instead of caving in and surrendering to it; as interfering children queued up to punch his head if they thought that they could get away with it (as they mostly could not).

He had not chosen their company, did not want it, and could not help having been born into it, so he took the view that he was in no way one of them and would never become one of them, as he took everything in his stride and kept his cool (another early character trait and development).

Robert could not believe all the trouble and strife to which he was subjected by other working-class, bully-boy children, merely because he insisted on speaking with a standard BBC/Oxford English accent that made them feel inferior for inferiority-complex reasons of their own (nothing to do with him!), not an accent with a plum or anything else snobby in his mouth, but simply a clearly well-spoken accent that would have been perfectly normal in a middle or upper class school.

Yet he was treated like a leper!

When they were the lepers – or the lunatics that were trying to take over the mental asylum!!

One might have thought, in view of all this, he would have finished up speaking his BBC/Oxford English awkwardly and self-consciously in an overly reactive lah-di-dah way, or through gritted and angry teeth of determination, but not at all, he took to standard English naturally like a duck to water and spoke it in a relaxed and free-flowing very natural way that was second nature to him, the only boy in the school whose beautiful spoken (and written) English stood out like a sore thumb!

In future years, many an attractive woman would fall for his spoken voice in addition to all else, and would tell him so, not that any of them ever knew how he had sweated metaphorical blood to speak as he did.

Because he was always – like his parents and two brothers – a handsome child and young man, in good physical condition and shape, he was usually spoilt for choice when it came to girlfriends and older female partners, with more than his fair share than most because, furthermore, he was full of easy-going charm and really could charm the birds from the trees.

It was in 1954 – the year of the Coronation Prize – that the novelist Kingsley Amis had his novel *Lucky Jim* ['I envy him!'] published before it was turned into a film later on. He was one of several so-called Angry Young Men novelists and playwrights whose works were yet to be published, performed and turned into films in due course, including *Look Back in Anger* and *The Entertainer* by John Osborne, the former of which transformed and modernised British theatre (it addressed Britain's purpose in the post-imperial age, and off-stage Osborne described his hated working-class cockney barmaid mother 'as my disease, my sick room'). It was also later on in near-future years that Alan Silitoe (the son of a working-class factory worker in Derby) wrote *The Loneliness of the Long Distance Runner* (Robert knew all about this from his own cross country running) *and Saturday Night and Sunday morning (*kitchen sink drama*)* whilst John Braine wrote *Life at The Top* and *Room at The Top*, all great and influential 'new wave' works of literature that Robert enjoyed before long.

Times they were a changing, but they had certainly taken their time and they could not change quickly enough for Robert.

Chapter Two: Televising the Queen's 1953 Coronation

In due course, Jacko Jackson was once again back in his study asking how Robert felt about winning the Queen Elizabeth II Coronation Prize!

In later years there was a forever long stream of consciousness in Robert's mind and memory about this prize, flashing backwards and forwards about how he felt about it, both back then and later on and also in the whenever-now in the long reach of time, three different points in time – then, later on and here and now, as and when they occurred – always shifting with the shifting *then and now sands of time*, and as far as he could clearly remember (he always had an excellent long-term memory) Robert's long-term impression was that he always felt very good about winning this prize (he did not doubt that an unfailing long-term *impression* could only have been be born of a once upon a distant time *actual reality and truth*).

Whilst there is, as we know or should know, Proustian involuntary memory triggered involuntarily and accidentally – in addition to voluntary memory that is no accident because it is actively and deliberately voluntarily searched for, recalled and ordered – whenever one or other of these two very different recollections came and continued to come to Robert he always felt good about them, which is why he replied to his headmaster: 'Well... I'm very pleased indeed, sir' (more pleased back then, of course, when there was so much else for him and most others not to be very pleased about!).

'But there is more good news because your Geography teacher tells me that he has shown your school work to this town's excellent grammar school that has offered you a place there – subject to a personal interview that you will sail through with flying colours, I have no doubt – so that you can do your O and A levels, with a view to your going on to university, and that really is splendid news, is it not? '

'It is if my mother allows me to go there, sir, she wants me to leave school early, as she did in her time, and get a job for some much-needed money, but Mr McKay is visiting our home to see if he can get her to give her permission. My mother and father left school at 11 and 12 years of age, so she is not a great fan of education, having got by without it herself, same as my father of course. She actually jokes that children are better off leaving school before higher education does them any harm! She thinks that higher education is for those that can afford it, not for others who cannot, most of whom don't need it anyway.'

'That is ridiculous, Robert.'

'That's what my father tells her, but let's hope that Mr McKay can persuade her.'

'Mr McKay is an excellent Geography teacher and one of our very best teachers of all and he tells me that he is most impressed with your work, that you are without doubt university material.'

'I like him a lot. If I get to university before I am through, I will always remember him and your good self, sir.'

'Quite right, too, and so you should, especially remembering him. He will tell your mother that you will have done her and your family proud when you go to the Grammar. And You will have done this school proud because you will have demonstrated that this is a school that is capable of occasionally turning out a literate child who really is an outstanding all-rounder, the latter in view of your Coronation Prize, additional to your going to the local Grammar and on to university. And of course you will have done your parents proud for the way in which they have brought you up, as well as having done yourself proud' (clearly, pride – personal and national, as opposed to shame – was an important matter when young Robert was growing up!).

'Thank you, sir, as it happens I am quietly proud.'

'That's good, modesty in all things, loudly proud is no good at all, apart from on the military parade ground, and even then it needs to be discreetly dignified and stylish with it, nothing vulgar. But all your accomplishments are no mean achievement for all concerned and not least for a lesser school of this kind. It's all-rounders of your kind that this country needs, which is why this is such a special prize with which to mark the coronation of our newly crowned Queen. Did your parents manage to find a television set somewhere so that you could watch the Queen's coronation on screen last year?'

'We have our own television, sir, the only one in the entire neighbourhood if not in any working-class neighbourhood in this and surrounding towns. So relatives and friends came to our house from miles around to watch it on screen.'

'Really, I thought that you lived in the gas-lit end of town where electricity had not yet been installed from the national grid.'

'Yes we do, but my father built his own electricity generator in our back garden – where our wartime air-raid shelter used to be – so he generates our electricity. Which is how we became the only house in the neighbourhood to have electricity.'

'But how could your father afford a television set?'

'He couldn't, so he built his own, and it works brilliantly.'

'How very enterprising and clever of your father to do this, such a brilliant man. He must know quite a lot about electrical theory and engineering.'

'Yes, he does, and he has taught himself everything he knows, including maths, from various text books, because he left school at eleven years of age, one year ahead of my mother at twelve years of age, so he had no choice but to teach himself.'

'That is truly admirable, Robert, what an excellent man and family. Probably, with higher education, he would have become an electronics or electrical engineer.'

'I think so, or an automobile or aeronautical engineer, perhaps, because he has also built his own racing car. He and I talk a lot about the sciences and engineering and he has even confided in me that he would have most wished to be a medical doctor, had he had the education for it.'

'How do you mean *confided* in you?'

'He is too embarrassed to let it be generally known – seeing as he is only a plasterer on building sites – for fear of people laughing at him and thinking him stupidly pretentious and way too big for his boots, which in reality he never is. I had to look up the word pretentious in the dictionary and show it to him to prove to him that he could never-ever be such a thing! To prove that there is nothing pretentious about knowing what one's abilities are and wishing that one had achieved them.'

Jacko Jackson told Robert: 'Your father clearly has aptitudes for the sciences and technology and it is such a shame that he could never fulfil his vocational dream of becoming a doctor, as he may very well have done, given half a chance.

Working-class children had to pass a school-leaving exam in his day, to make sure they had at least a rudimentary, very basic education, before sending them on their way, and those that left school early at 11 years of age, like your father, were the bright ones who could pass the exam early. Those that left later at 12 or 13 years needed longer to pass the exam. Most left at 12.'

Sending them on their way with a flea in their ear, is what Robert thought of this, as he replied: 'So I have heard, sir.'

'Because the British economy has needed underpaid industrial workers, labourers and ordinary non-commissioned soldiers and sailors in the armed forces, there hasn't been much demand for too many educated people, which is why it has fallen to the bulk of the working-classes to leave school at eleven or twelve years of age, instead of becoming properly educated and going on to higher education like the middle and upper classes. But things should change for the better before long, as the economy and society take off, so we now have high hopes for you Robert if you carry on as you are, keeping up with and sometimes ahead of your studies.'

'Thank you, sir. I mean to find an escape route out of the working class. I have never thought that I *belonged* in this social class. I have been with it but not of it and through no fault of my own (as we see, Robert was quite a precocious child with his own very clear idea of who he was and could become, with his own self-worth and self-confidence very early on in life, and he was always the optimist who believed that he could and would overcome, correcting all the mistakes in his life (not just his spellings) that needed to be corrected and put right and learning what he needed to learn, following his father's own good electrical and automobile example in this respect).'

'Of course you do and I am sure that you will. You are a square peg in a round hole here in this school in which you are wasted, which is absolutely why you really must go to the Grammar........So you saw the Queen's coronation on television? That does surprise me. Yours is a family that is full of very pleasing surprises, Robet...... Did you know that the coronation almost did not get televised?'

'I heard some rumours.'

'The reason was that the Archbishop of Canterbury and other establishment figures, including Winston Churchill, our former wartime prime minister, were opposed to it and they almost but not quite persuaded the former Princess Elizabeth to disallow the intrusive television cameras into Westminster Abbey so that the nation could see her crowned. They thought it would set a very disturbing precedent, allowing pesky cameras to be included in royal affairs in the so-called public interest. They wanted to keep the coronation a private and exclusive affair for the few thousand VIP guests who were invited to sit in the Abbey and witness the ceremony.'

'I am glad it was televised, sir.'

'The privileged few argued that the mystique of royalty would be blown sky-high and gone for ever once television got its teeth into our monarchs and their families, believing that the cameras would be the death of monarchy if we don't watch out. And so it will of old-style monarchy, I shouldn't wonder! But we must move with the times for all that, there's no point inventing television and then not using it too good effect. Monarchy must move with the times, same as everybody else, and the Queen and her husband have recognised this, even though there will inevitably be privacy difficulties and problems along the way. But her advisors said let the public hear about the wedding on the wireless [radio] and read about it in the newspapers, but don't let them see it, let them not be included with the great and the good who are so very highly privileged to witness the ceremony with their own eyes. Their attitude was - keep the public at arm's length and let them continue to have a peek-a-boo relationship with monarchy. Don't let the cameras be in the faces of our royals. But the new Queen would hear nothing of it, so she and her husband the Duke of Edinburgh stood their ground and insisted on her coronation being televised – to a staggering 20 million viewers, would you believe?'

'Gosh! That's a lot of viewers.'

'It is the first time in our history that a coronation has been televised or that this country has had the means to do it, so it broke new ground, because it seems that Queen Elizabeth II is a progressive and modern, new-look monarch, not one of the old school. But I am glad that you and your family managed to see it on your own television screen, thanks to your enterprising and progressive father. Perhaps we should give him a prize also!'

'He's a very modest man, but I expect he wouldn't mind a coronation prize if one came his way.'

'Unfortunately he's not likely to get one, but I am in favour of prizes myself. I think they motivate people to do better and keep up their good work, and they remind others of the good work that needs to be done, which they can also do if they exert themselves, as they and we all need to do.'

Although television had been invented in1926 (thirteen years before Robert's birth in 1939 at the outbreak of World War Two), it had taken another twenty years before the first TV-transmission took place in Britain at Alexander Palace in North London in 1946, and another twenty-seven years from the time of its invention for it to seriously get going in 1950s Britain. This was because it had been delayed, first by a lack of investment - and also a lack of retail potential for mass production, given that most people could not afford to buy a television - and then by the interruption of the war years and their ruinous economic aftermath, as explained in the previous chapter.

When Robert was born in 1939, Prince Philip, the Queen's husband, attended Dartmouth College in Devonshire in the West of England in order to train as a naval officer in the British Navy, which was the year that war broke out, and when it did so, it put back the development of television and much else in Britain.

Robert was born an aforesaid 'war baby' on 11.9.39 at the outset of war, which was not at all a good time to be born!

Like Robert's mother and father, neither the Queen nor her husband had been to university, but they had received an excellent preparatory and senior education, the Queen from private tutors in her palatial home, and Philip at the best schools that prepared him for a naval career rather than a university education, and they did have very well-spoken English voices with posh accents. Philip was always the modernizer in the British royal family, urging his wife to modernize as well.

Robert's had been an accidental birth because his mother – in her late forties – had been told by her doctor that she was suddenly of an infertile age at which she could no longer become pregnant, so she and her husband stopped taking birth control precautions for the first time in their married life, as a result of which Robert dropped from his mother's womb accidentally and unexpectedly into a working-class life that was full of unexpected accidents for better or worse, usually the latter.

Not until the early 1960s – at least thirty-four years after its invention - did television really get into gear as a popular news and entertainments channel for the masses, with a television set in virtually every home. Slow progress indeed.

The head repeated to Robert 'you really are lucky to have a television in your home, Robert, the working classes don't usually have TV. They make do with wireless instead.'

The same was true of cars and motorbikes. The working classes had generally 'made do' with pedalling their bicycles, except for Robert's family. Robert's father had built his own racing car from spare parts, the brakes of which failed on one occasion, causing his car to collide with the chauffeur-driven *Rolls Royce* of the chairman of the town's famous biscuit factory that became 'royally appointed' when British royals took a liking to the biscuits and started to eat them at tea time with cups of tea and also took them with them on their tours abroad.

Shortly after crashing his racing car, Robert's father acquired a cheap second-hand saloon car – a *Flying Standard* - that nobody wanted because it was in need of much repair, but this suited him just fine because he knew how to repair it with spare parts and how to transform it into a very comfortable, highly polished, family car, of which to be proud. So he soon graduated from bicycling to work, with his tool kit and lunch pack on his back for many a long mile, to motor cars and also to motor bikes. He was a man who could turn his hand to almost anything mechanical or electrical, with a passion for motorised vehicles and also for speed (all of the cars in those colourless days were black). His younger sons Robert and Laurence became really fast drivers, with Robert doing some rallying and racing in an *MG Sports* and *Ford Mustang* and eventually having a son who became a part-time motor racing driver and champion.

'We have a wireless also,' Robert told his headmaster, 'made by my father from spare parts, and I love to listen to the comedy programmes on Sunday afternoons – *Educating Archie*, the *Goons*, *Take it from Here* and *The Glums*.'

'Yes, the *Goon Show* in particular, is very funny. That's something else we need much more of in this country, much more comedy, wit and humour, in addition to more all-rounders.'

'What I like about listening to radio is that you have to use your imagination more than watching television in which next to nothing is left to the imagination because it is all so very visual.'

'That's right and very well observed Robert.'

Robert's hard-working and long-suffering father really was an inspirational example to his sons. Life was always interesting and amazing when he was around with all his new inventions that occupied his time at the end of a long working day on the building sites and otherwise at weekends after a hard working week, and his secret ambition for being a medical doctor clearly resulted from his treating all the wounds in his family home, administering ointments and bandaging cuts and bruises, including the cracked veins in the legs of Robert's grandma on his mother's side whose legs were so painful after giving birth to so many children and toiling long and hard at her housework all day, that the poor woman bumped herself down the stair on her posterior, because she could no longer walk.

The working classes rarely saw doctors in those unenviable pre and post second-world-war times leading to the 1950s and 1960s when Britain's National Health Service was not more than a fledgling with a long way to go.

The small working-class, red-brick terrace house where Robert lived with his parents and his elder brother Roy, thirteen years Robert's senior - soon to be joined by a third, younger brother, to be called Laurence, five years behind Robert, and also consigned to a rubbish secondary school - was a typical house in a downmarket neighbourhood in a railway cum country market town in the Southeast of England (a major junction for trains heading north, south, east and west, that was scheduled to grow into a really large town in due course), and during Robert's formative years there had been a zinc bathtub in this house, hanging on a rusty nail in the back yard (a small yard magically transformed into a beautiful little garden by Robert's green-fingered mother).

In the absence of a bathroom, this zinc tub had been hauled, once a week, into a scullery at the back of the premises where the dishes were washed. The scullery also passed for a kitchen and bathroom combined, where food was cooked for all meals and where Robert and Roy had been bathed and scrubbed weekly by their mother, after she had filled the tub with warm water that was heated in buckets on a gas oven, before being poured into the tub.

The house also had an outside toilet at the bottom of the back garden. But, as we have heard, Robert's father soon demolished this inconvenient loo when he converted a coal shed adjacent to the scullery and made it part of the inside of the house - by putting his protective overhead roof between the shed and the rear roof of the house and also some side walls to go with it – so that this shed became an enclosed part of the back of the house, more readily accessible, warmer and a much more comfortable inside toilet that was sparklingly clean and modern.

Of course he also had to do all the plumbing, drainage and pipe work, in order to install the toilet inside the shed, not that this deterred him in the least.

In due course Robert's younger brother Laurence knew nothing of all this, because he was born later when times had improved immeasurably, but Robert and Roy grew up in this way. At the same time, Laurence was denied a grammar school education, as he went to a secondary-old technical school instead that held him back, as he left school without a single qualification to his name, staring his first job as a garage mechanic (whereas Robert's first jobs were in journalism for the local newspaper and thereafter for a law firm as an articled clerk, called 'paralegal' later on).

Because Roy was thirteen years older than Robert, he was very much the big brother, but he soon went away to war, to fight the Japanese in Burma, but not before teaching Robert how to swim and play football and also how to box (as did, more decisively, Robert's father, given that he was a former amateur boxer who had turned down an offer to turn professional).

Robert's headmaster told him: 'It is because you are by far the most adventurous and public-spirited pupil in this school that it has come as no surprise to me that you have won this Coronation Prize, Robert.'

'Thank you, sir, but it never previously occurred to me that I had done so much for the local community.'

'On the contrary. You have written and acted in two of your own school plays for parent's evenings - when parents and others in the local community have all come to the school to see them - which is more than most children of your age have done. That is the work you have done for your community. And you have also represented the wider community in the county of Berkshire, in the Schools National Cross-Country Championships at Heaton Park in Manchester, which was televised, when you came 50th out of 250 runners, as I recall. Heaton Park is real torture territory for cross country running, on account of its very steep and very long hill that schoolboys had to run up. I hear that you could have done much better had you not stayed up most of the night in a Manchester jazz club near the Heaton Lads Club - where your team stayed over - on the eve of the day before the race! Goodness knows what you were thinking of, but no matter, you still managed to do well enough, and this is another reminder of the all-rounder you are. You stay out late enjoying jazz, yet still do pretty well in a cross country race the following morning. You also won the Berkshire 100-mile cycle race over the Berkshire Downs and beyond. 50th out of 250 in a national cross-country race is not at all bad, after jazzing your legs off all night.'

'49th sir.'

'Very well, 49th, even better. And you have participated in school camps during your holidays, helping to make them a success, while also representing your school in rowing, football, athletics, swimming and boxing all in the local community, and in each of which you have won your house colours. School camps are very important for community spirit and also good for the morale of families that cannot afford to take their children on holiday on account of the war years, and you have led the way encouraging children to come to camp, pitching tents, digging the latrines and so on. You have led by example in the community and given this school the lead in several sports. You are a house captain, setting a good example to others and taking responsibility for them. You are not only a Berkshire cycle-racing champion, but a member of the Youth Hostels Association, cycling for hundreds and thousands of miles all over this country during school holidays and at weekends, and also into Europe on the last occasion when I understand that you cycled to Germany and Belgium staying in youth hostels in those countries.

'Yes, it was quite an adventure, sir.'

'Youth hostels are no less important to community spirit in this country when there's not much else for children to do or places for them to go. So this went all in your favour when you deservedly won this prize. Your infectious passion and optimism has been an inspiration to us all and not least to those in the community – you could not have been more public spirited.

'I see. I never thought of that.'

Many of these children and their parents to whom Robert has been an inspiration – including Robert himself – really had been brought up to be more modest than they needed to be and to underrate or understate their achievements. This is how working-class children were brought up in those days by their parents, grandparents and school teachers. They were not encouraged to think highly of themselves or of their achievements, but to play the latter down rather. But Robert's head master was one of those who had been with Winston Churchill when he had said of the post-war prime minister Clement Attlee – a proudly modest man – that Atlee had 'a lot to be modest about!'

'Getting out of the towns and cities into the countryside and getting plenty of fresh air, keeping fit while cycling hundreds of miles, and improving one's map reading in order to find one's way round the country, is a very good way of lifting spirits and giving children something to aim for and look forward to. In all this you have been a pioneering and inspirational example to other children, Robert, cycling long distances to London, Oxford, Bristol, Stratford-upon-Avon and back again, I hear. I also hear that you and your friends have cycled as far as Land's End in Cornwall and all the way back again.'

'Yes, another adventure, but on British soil this time sir.'

'That is quite amazing and an excellent way of getting children out and about. And, what is more, your class work is not at all bad, to go with all your other credentials for this prize. You have an excellent record, which is why we have such high hopes for you in the fullness of time. I am told that you are getting top marks for English Language and Literature, History and Geography and passable marks for Maths and Commerce, the latter of which can lead to the study of Economics should you decide to go in that direction. All things considered, Robert, I can think of no better person for a prize of this kind.'

'Thank you, sir.'

'I doubt that there is any other pupil in this town who has done more than you for his school or its local community, especially when entertaining it with his plays. That's what this prize is all about – showing an affinity with others and sharing a sense of community and community spirit with them, getting out there and doing things for your school, rather than just sitting in the classroom and being a swot all the time. Yes, we want people who can use their brains, but we also want public spirited people with good all-round abilities and self-reliant and resilient character development, people who will muck in and not shirk or shrink from doing their bit. You have shown plenty of character, so well done. Well done indeed. If we don't encourage good character development in this country, how can we expect people to be of good character? Not many people are born with good or strong characters, they have to learn this and work at it, and if we don't teach it by example, it will simply disappear, and we shall breed generations of feeble people without any backbone or character whatsoever.'

'Very good point, sir.'

'You think so, do you? Well, I'm very pleased to hear it. The object of this prize is to restore public spirit and improve morale, which has taken a bit of a battering since the war, and also to lift the spirits of parents, teachers and school children alike, giving them all some pride in the achievements of our ablest and inspirational pupils. You have real leadership qualities, Robert. You are a natural-born leader, popular with your teachers and the envy of your fellow pupils.

You always take the lead and the bull by the horns and that is very good and inspirational for other pupils. You show the way. Character development absolutely is all-important and I can see that your character is shaping up and developing very well. The more you live actively, the more you can learn actively, and as long as you do continue to live and learn, it looks like your character is turning out very well indeed. You and your character will change and you will finish up not the person you were, but the improved person that you have become, which is what character development is all about, learning and becoming a fully developed human being, not some one- dimensional shallow person, or a lopsided single-ability person, but a fully rounded person – a generalist, no less. And I must say that your leadership qualities are excellent.'

The headmaster was getting really carried away now (as was Robert listening to all this guff and high praise!), this head who could not resist banging the drum for all-rounders.

This was not a headmaster who praised people – especially children – very often or even at all, because he too often found them to be lazy good for nothings of whom he was highly critical, being a hard task master who did not believe in praising those that did not earn it or deserve it, and even then not overdoing it, as a matter of principle. So this was praise indeed from such a man.

But Jacko 'the Jackson' also believed in giving credit where it was due, especially when he heard to his exasperation that Robert had mixed feelings about leadership, 'for heaven's sake and whatever next!'

He had already told Robert that: 'There are those that can make good leadership speeches and promises, but turn out to be bad leaders, and others who are no good at the speeches or promises, but turn out to be good if not excellent leaders. For these reasons, leadership can easily fall into the hands of feeble fools or tricksters and go badly wrong, which is why we must all have a hand in leadership whether we like it or not. As a former Royal Navy officer in wartime, I know what I'm talking about, and I must say that I rather enjoy leading people for the better rather than leaving them to their own devices for the worse. I know a good leader when I see one and will do what I can to help him as best I can.'

But Robert insisted that he really hadn't set out to 'lead' anybody.

On the contrary, he pointed out that his house captainship had been thrust upon him – he was captain of *Kennet House*, named after one of the three rivers around which his home town was built – and this captaincy had been thrust upon him as a result of his having got himself into some leadership positions when he had taken the initiative at school and on the sports field, taking matters into his own hands simply because nobody else had shown any interest. Almost absent-mindedly, one might say, he had become a leader when others neglected or failed to do so.

To which his headmaster replied: 'Which is why you are a natural-born leader,' leaving Robert to speculate and think out loud, 'whether people are worth leading?'

Jacko Jackson's typical answer to this was: 'Of course many if not most people are not worth leading, which is precisely why we have to lead them before some other far worse leader gets his or her hands on them. But just because they are not worth leading – usually because they are so stupid or lazy – this doesn't mean that they will not be gullible enough to stupidly follow and be led by the nose by someone even more stupid than themselves. We cannot leave them to the leadership of idiots and undesirables. We have to lead them whether we like it or not.'

But, young as he was, Robert already had his doubts about this and he much preferred people to lead themselves - on the other hand, could they be relied upon to do so, as Jacko doubted that they could? In fact, Jacko was adamant that they could not and Robert had a vague suspicion that he may be right.

In which case, one had to take the initiative in order to get things done and manage them when nobody else would, which was when one inevitably became a leader, without necessarily wanting the responsibility.

And Robert realised that there was a big difference between getting things done and then managing them thereafter when they could be undone by bad managers!

At the same time, Robert was no control freak in the making, and he much preferred to give people their own heads if he could, and he did not like giving orders or bossing others around. He had become a house captain prematurely in his earlier teens because there were no fifteen-year-olds ahead of him who wanted or were worthy of the position. But he would be leaving school very soon now, unless his mother allowed him to stay on at the Grammar (his father was already in agreement, but his mother remained to be convinced, and she was nothing if not a hard woman to convince of anything that she doubted).

It is perfectly true that Robert – who was not destined, as things turned out, to become a future leader of men in the fullness of time – led his house in all sorts of ways as a house captain and that he had inspired a handful of his friends to follow him into post-war Germany and Belgium during the long summer holidays (six weeks), cycling all the way there and back again. They stayed in a youth hostel in Germany, in the mountain district of Monchau Eiffel, where Robert and his cycling colleagues attended the famous *Carousel Carnival*, when he danced in the streets with an unknown young German girl who seemed to be of his own age, with her memorable curly blonde hair, pretty face, blue eyes and pretty carnival dress.

As it happened, Prince Philip, Queen Elizabeth's husband, had been schooled in Germany before he arrived in Britain, where he had German-Danish family, and with pre-war photographs of him when in school there showed him to be a typical blonde-haired, blue-eyed very German-looking child. He had a reputation for being a boisterous child who is supposed to have un-typically roared with laughter when children in his school were required give the Nazi salute after Hitler came to power and before Philip came to Britain – laughing at the nonsense and folly of it all, while straight-face others in Germany took it very seriously and believed it all.

So what kind of leader was Hitler?

The wrong leader for all the wrong reasons, of course.

Being of a generation whose parents had fought a vicious and narrowly victorious war against the Germans – a hard-fought war that came close to being almost lost to these Germans – Robert and his friends were curious to go and see for themselves what these hated Germans were like, so they cycled all the way to their former enemy's country, and when they got there, they were surprised to find most of them hospitable and friendly and not unlike the British in several respects, and how absurd was that?

From a young age, Robert really did find himself, developing a peculiar sense of the absurd, for which he could not exactly find the right words at the time, but for which he nevertheless had a strong feeling that there was indeed something completely absurd about the world and its people and history, killing each other one moment, and being chummy the next. With British governments welcoming

Scottish royals to join their royal club - to prevent the English and Scots from hating and killing each other - and then welcoming German royals for the same reasons!

This sense of the absurd that was developing in Robert's mind, not only applied to warfare and the historical tensions and hatreds between Britain and Germany, but it also applied, in due course, inevitably to the absurdities of British royals (yet he had also learned that there was nothing absurd about their Coronation prize that he was very pleased to win because made a lot of sense).

When Robert and his cycling friends left Germany and reached Brussels - the capital city of Belgium on their way back to Britain - they found that there was no room for them in the youth hostel there because it was full of Belgian children, so they were re-directed to a monastery in Bruges instead, where the monks kindly took them in late at night and gave them a bed. When they arrived at the monastery after dark, and knocked on its ancient wooden doors, the monks were astonished to find a bunch of kids from England who had cycled all the way to Belgium, but they did not hesitate to give them a meal and a bed for the night. Robert and his friends were no less astonished to find that the monks were gambling – playing cards – and drinking wine!

The following morning, after breakfast in a large dining hall, these robed monks stood in line, in a long queue, holding their used breakfast plates, mugs and cutlery, waiting in turn to wash them in a kitchen sink, before going on their way.

And while they queued in this fashion - in their dark-brown hooded robes - they swayed and jigged and jived around to jazz music that was played on an old piano by a fellow monk (perhaps they were happy that Europe was no longer at war and that liberated Belgium was no longer occupied by Hitler's Germany).

Robert and his friends also stood in line to wash up in this way, before taking their leave and thanking these kindly monks for their hospitality.

Clearly, Robert and his generation were mostly nothing if not adventurous and, as we see from his various activities in and out of school, there was a lot of precocity in his young life. He was an ambitious and enterprising young child, and engaging with it, and he intended to make his way in this world, not on the building sites like his father before him, as his mother (but not his father) wished, but in one of the white-collar professions instead. He wasn't sure how he was going to do this exactly, but he was certainly going to find out how and give it his best shot – how to find a way to make something of himself. He wasn't going to settle for being an office boy, a clerk, or a travelling salesman, or anything like that, he was going to aim far higher. Probably his mother, who did not have her son's confidence or enterprise, thought this was all pie in the sky, which is why she wished for the only certainties that she knew, one of which was building trade work in plastering in the footsteps of her husband for her sons (on the other hand, Robert's elder brother Roy had found a white collar clerical job, not that it paid him very much).

Robert's headmaster told him: 'You still have a lot of growing up to do, Robert, but I repeat that you are developing well at present, with a fine balance between your performance in the class room and your performance on the sports field - not to mention your work in the community - so keep it up, you're doing well. I've noticed that you don't waste your time hanging out with the children in this school who are, alas, a bad influence and are going nowhere, and I would keep it that way if I were you.'

'Thank you, sir, I will.'

It was perfectly true that, as the head had suggested, Robert's character was developing all the time and swiftly so (not all children have notably or swiftly developing characters), and as it did so he was learning more and more and becoming a changed person very much for the better, but he was determined not to let this or this Coronation Prize go to his head.

But what a head-start he was getting, and how he was learning fast and changing fast, and all to the good.

And Robert was by no means finished yet.

He was poised for much more character development to follow in later years (but that is another story for another time), after everything he had packed into his early life, without giving it too much reflective thought, seeing as he had been too busy doing and enjoying it all and getting it all done than to reflect on it.

Reflective thought was triggered much later in his life, as it so often is, when he began to wonder why he was as he was and who he was, and how he had arrived at the person that he was (this was thought that was not infrequently provoked by others who observed the kind of person that he was and commented on it, favourably for the most part).

He found it very interesting to consider what triggers reflective thought in people young and old – conversations and comparisons with others, as well as those conversations that reflective thinkers have with themselves under their breath and in their inner-minds? – and why some of us are much more contemplative and reflective than others.

Whilst some young people hardly ever reflected at all – especially the children of his working-class neighbours and also his fellow working-class school children, as he soon discovered when he overhead their conversations – Robert was not one of them; which is perhaps not surprising, seeing as there was such a lot that he wanted to change for the better for himself in his life, in his determination to escape from his working-class origins, cut them off at the roots and put them behind him. By contrast they did not want to change themselves or their class, but just carry on as they were.

Robert wanted out of the working class, not because he was ashamed of its humble origins in any way (not at all and perish the thought!), but simply because they were origins that were not a good or natural fit for him as they evidently were for others who were content with their class, as a result of which he had a lot to think about!

Why was he not like the rest of them?

Why did he stick out like a sore thumb?

How best to change his class and get ahead?

How come these origins suited others when they did not suit him?

What was wrong with these others (or with him!)?

There was so much for him to think about, just as his father thought a lot about electrical theory and *ohms law* in order to understand it better and learn how to invent and generate some electricity in his home to make it a better dwelling place for his family.

Robert reached the conclusion that he and his father were the thinkers in their family, his dad thinking intelligently about how to improve their lot under the roof of their house (and also in his self-employed workplace by working hard to make enough money to survive), while Robert thought about how to improve himself educationally for a better life away from such a house in its working-class community, in the fullness of time.

Unlike the aforementioned Angry Young Man playwright, John Osborne – who hated his working-class barmaid cockney mother, as we have heard already (he who was the son of a Welsh commercial artist and advertising copywriter) – Robert did not hate his mother (on the contrary he loved her), but she was a thorn in his flesh when it came to his breaking loose from his class and going to grammar school and university (he was learning how to love a thorn in his flesh and this was quite a challenge!).

Robert certainly loved his mother, but he did not like her misguided terms, or intend to accept them, as he viewed her philosophically and sympathetically with pity and understanding of where she was coming from, rather than hate. So there was plenty of friction in his relationship with her that meant that he got on a lot better with his father. His mother's handwriting was all over Robert's elder brother, and also his younger brother Laurence, rather than him, and not least all over Laurence because he had no great educational ambitions of which she disapproved and had every intention of leaving school with all possible speed regardless of whether he was suitably qualified or not.

Laurence also looked a lot more like his mother and her family, so he had this chemistry in his favour with her, for which she did not hesitate to spoil him something rotten, which was fine with Robert, given that he was a lot closer to his father and not only looked more like him and his family, but thought more like his father than his mother.

101

In future years, one of Robert's favourite poems became *This Be the Verse* by the poet Larkin: 'They fuck you up, your mum and dad, they may not mean to but they do, they give you all the faults they had, and add some extra just for you.'

Through no particular fault of their own – before this 1960s poem was written and published - 1940s and 1950s mums and dads inherited a lot of faults from their very peculiar and unjust history, social system and culture that later generations did not inherit, and there were plenty of 'extras' to be added as well, from that period of time, before this poem caught the popular imagination.

Also in future years, Robert would become a great fan of the aforementioned John Osborne and his plays and he wondered if this playwright's mother had been really nasty and spiteful to her yet to be famous son for him to have hated her so much.

In relation to his father, as we have seen, Robert's thought was more sociological, philosophical and sophisticated – when it came to grasping and understanding the background to his and his parents' lowly circumstances - whilst his father's thought was more practical, vocational and scientific as he got on with the business of improving their lot as best he could within the limits that applied to their situation.

There were two very different kinds of thought for two very similar thinkers here, always thinking with improvement and self-improvement in mind, of one kind or another, always reasoning and logically deducing what needed to be reasoned and logically deduced (and both with a great sense of humour, as it happened!).

Not that either of these different kinds of thought were ever put into writing, not Robert's because he was too young to have the vocabulary to write anything more than a short schoolboy essay or one of his school plays – he was far from the fully-fledged writer that he hoped to become in his adult life – and certainly not his father's thought because he was a largely illiterate man who had, as we have heard, left school at 11-years-of-age and did not have the education and literacy for writing such a 'think-piece.' He could do what he could do, but not put it into words. There was instinctive and observational learning in the family, but nothing, as yet, sufficiently literary for the purpose of getting it all written (for which reason Robert was beginning to think that perhaps he should become a journalist when he grew up). Robert also had an instinctive intuition for reading and judging people's characters, which he was yet to learn was the big thing that English Literature had to offer.

On reflection in later years, Robert thought that he had learned most in his young life from his cycling and youth hostelling which, apart from the obvious physical exercise, was one big geography and social studies lesson, learned from personal experience and observation and map reading.

Before he took to the road on his bicycle in his early teenage years, he did not know about all the places he was able to visit and how much they differed. Nor did he meet all the very different sorts of children from all over the country, including some outside the country in the aforementioned Germany and Belgium, until he stayed in youth hostels, and he did not learn all the things that he learned about geography and map reading either, meeting so many different people in different towns, villages, cities and regions on two continents.

So Robert was not just developing his schoolboy muscles physically by cycling his vast distances, but his educational, sociological and psychological muscles as well, in relation to so many different people and places and how to read them differently and deal with them and understand them differently (most of which was a big bore to his mother, but not his father who was fascinated to hear Robert's accounts of all his journeys).

Had he not taken to the road on his bike and learned how to fend for himself at home and abroad, Robert's stay-at-home character would not have developed in this way, enabling him to become such an outgoing character. In fact he would have been a very different, more parochial and narrow, less adventurous or knowledgeable and less worldly-wise person, for one so young. He would have been much more insular.

The same could be said of his school camps and the writing of his school plays. So he really was developing and changing all the time and at the rate of knots. And the same could also be said, furthermore, for his increasing knowledge of his extraordinary and inspirational headmaster, who had been quite a distant and forbidding person before Robert was nominated for his Coronation prize and went on to win it. For sure, Robert was learning and indeed developing fast, streets ahead of most children his age. There was a tonne of character development for him that was going on in his life.

Not that Robert realised all this while he was at school.

Nor had he heard that it had been Richard Schirrman, a German school teacher, who had founded the world's first youth hostel in 1909, five years before World War One in 1914. This hostel was for young people from poor families living in large industrial cities and inner-city slums, with hardly any money in their pockets, to escape from their environmental misery and enjoy the countryside, by renting a very cheap bed for the night in low-cost but decent and cheerful, clean accommodation, in healthy rural surroundings, breathing fresh country air, perhaps for the first time in their lives.

By the time Robert's generation came along in the aftermath of World War Two, this youth hostel idea had spread to the UK where the Youth Hostels Association (YHA) was going strong, providing much-needed clean and airy, basic accommodation, in country cottages, houses, mansions, castles and other buildings that had been gifted to the YHA, which was linked with hostels abroad. Unless one lives in a polluted industrial city – or in a smoky and dusty coal-fired, gas-lit house, with no air-conditioning (as Robert did) – one cannot begin to imagine the significance of clean fresh air.

Robert's mother understood it perfectly, which is why she opened all her windows daily, in the coldest and dampest of weathers, to give her house an airing, and not least in the early mornings when she opened her children's bedroom windows to encourage them to get out of bed: 'This window stays open wide until you lazy children get out of bed, get washed and dressed and come down stairs and have your breakfast.'

'But it's absolutely freezing in here now.'

'Of course it is and it's all your own fault for not getting out of bed the first time I called you. I have other things to do than to stand around pleading with you to get out of bed in the morning. Your breakfast is made and going cold, so hurry up. If you're not out of bed within five minutes I shall come and throw a bucket of cold water over you.'

As we see, Robert's mother had her own leadership qualities!

This was quite a normal parental and loving way of talking to and treating working-class children in those days and it was not regarded as personal or in any way offensive or intimidating, and this is because it was not, of course, either of these things. Robert and his elder brother Roy giggled at the thought of their mother throwing a bucket of cold water over them, as they got out of bed shivering and climbing into their clothes.

Breakfast was usually piping-hot porridge or some other cereal, or if you were lucky, a fried egg and bacon once in a while. Robert's father usually consumed jam sandwiches and a small pot of tea (in an aluminium pot) before going to work, with a packet of cheese and onion sandwiches for his lunch.

To have cycled the length and breadth of England for hundreds and thousands of miles was quite a feat for a fourteen-year-old schoolboy in 1950s England, but that's what many children did in those days, when Robert thought nothing of cycling 80 or 100 miles a day to youth hostels to such destinations as Bristol or Stratford-upon-Avon (where he visited the Royal Shakespeare theatre in the latter town) as previously mentioned, or on return journeys to London, Portsmouth or Southampton. And it was perfectly true that he had also cycled for thousands of miles all the way to Land's End and back, stopping of at different hostels in Dorset, Devon and Cornwall, all very scenic places that he would not have been able to see otherwise, because he would not have been able to afford it.

It stands to reason that such determined children were in robust health and very self-confident, resourceful and mature, with plenty of physical stamina. But they were also modest because they were brought up to be so, so they did not pin medals on themselves for their enterprise and determination, and nor did their parents, so it had not previously occurred to Robert that there was anything special or remarkable about any of these things that he had done, innocently enough for pleasure rather than for glory, and to please himself rather than anybody else, to lead himself rather than to lead anybody else or be led by them.

In fact, it had not previously occurred to him that he had done so many things, because he had not been counting. But listening to the headmaster, he was reminded that he had been very active outside school, not only in the local community, but nationally and internationally as well, so it began to dawn on him that maybe there was something in what the head had to say. Maybe Robert was reasonably outstanding. Even though, in his deadpan way, he had thought nothing of his achievements before (at a time in British history when children were not encouraged to think much of their achievements for fear of them becoming 'too big for their boots' or 'too big headed'). But perhaps he had been setting a good and inspirational example.

If it were not for his Coronation Prize, none of this would have occurred to Robert, or would have been known to anyone else for that matter (just as this tory would not have been written). Whilst none of this would have occurred to him. It would have happened to him just the same, but it would not have been acknowledged, and it was this acknowledgement that brought on the thought-provoking and possibly life-changing occurrence that very probably spurred him on with swifter and greater resolution.

Without this prize, all his efforts would have passed unrecognised and Robert was about to go and share this thought with his headmaster - later on, on some other day - but was pre-empted when, yet again, Jacko Jackson suddenly called him to his study, for who knows what this time?

Chapter Three: Book Tokens from The Queen

'Come in, Robert, and take a seat my boy. Your prize has finally arrived – your book tokens from the Queen of England. A truly historic moment for you and this school. This school and one of its pupils has never been honoured with a present from the Queen before. This is going to make your day, as it is mine. Such a jolly day that will never be forgotten.'

Robert's face was beaming and gleaming brightly, same as Jacko Jackson's: 'A jolly good day indeed, sir.'

'What a way to start a day, with a present from the Queen of England. I envy you Robert and am so very pleased for you.'

'Thank you, sir'

Because the headmaster was usually a remote, no-nonsense and authoritarian figure, who did not encourage too much familiarity with his pupils, Robert had never seen him so relaxed and happy before., this head who was a very stern disciplinarian, who did not believe that all you had to do was to love children to get the best out of them. On the contrary, he was an exponent of tough love who believed that all you had to do was to discipline them! He believed in parent and teacher power, not pupil power, and in tough love, not any other kind. However, Robert was now discovering another, warmer side to him that was very congenial, and is was another side to his character that he was very pleased to know.

This headmaster's subjects were maths, science and the classics, about which he seemed to know a great deal, and he could chalk up mathematical calculations on a blackboard at the rate of knots, to the bewilderment of most children (and other teachers!). He ran a good and well-disciplined school in which the pupils were generally not seriously unhappy, even though he did not hesitate to cane them when they misbehaved, as they frequently did.

There were no pupils bullying teachers in those days, or daring to attack them, not because such pupils did not exist, but because they – and also their parents – were not tolerated.

Most male teachers – and notably the headmaster – did not suffer fools gladly and they knew how to stand their ground against violent and disruptive pupils, including their belligerent parents, both of whom were kept in their place and not allowed to disturb the peace and learning of others, as they often tried to do.

'There are two book tokens here that have just arrived for you from the W.H.Smith book chain in the centre of town, for you to go there and choose one or two books.'

'I can't wait, sir.'

111

'Good, so go straight away and enjoy your winnings. You can take the morning off school and take your time. It's a good thing to get children reading as much as possible. Do you have many books in your home?

'Afraid not, sir. We don't have too much money for such luxuries as books and, during my first five to ten years, there has not been much time for reading on account of the war, the air raids, and following the war daily on the radio, day and night. So this is a useful prize to me. We have a dictionary that I regularly consult to get my spellings right.'

'I suppose now that those wartime days are behind you, you borrow books from the lending library?'

'Yes, that's right.'

'But you must have a bible in your home, surely?'

'Not even that. We're not a very religious household, sir.'

'But you go to Sunday School and one of your uncles on your mother's side is a Sunday School teacher.'

'That's right, but the only reason that our and most other parents send us to Sunday School is to give them a rest from their children on Sunday afternoons.'

112

'So your parents not read children's stories to you when you were younger, before you went to bed?'

'Not when I was born, not in 1939.'

'I suppose not. Too busy with the war effort, hiding in cold and damp underground air-raid shelters in the back garden at bedtime and/or during the night, sitting in the dark with nothing more than a candle or a torch and a blanket, no doubt. But you do like books?'

'Very much so, and English Literature is a favourite subject of mine, and my mother and grandfather get library books from the public library. But the only books in our house have been the very useful technical books that explain to my father how to make things and do things. My father does everything in the house, from sweeping the chimneys to repairing our shoes and doing all the plumbing and decorating and fixing the electrics after he has come home from work and had a quick cup of tea and a quick read of the newspaper.'

'What newspaper does he read?'

'The *Daily Express*. He says it's rubbish, but that it has the best sports pages, which is why he buys it. My mother says she couldn't care less about newspapers. She reads her library books instead – romantic fiction – Barber Cartland which my father also says is rubbish!'

'The right-wing *Daily Express* and romantic fiction! Now there's a thought....... The *Express* has the biggest circulation in the country I believe. Some 2.5 million copies every day. A million copies more than the left-wing *Daily Mirror* and the right-wing *Daily Mail*. I hear from your geography teacher, Mr McKay, that it's your ambition to be a journalist?'

'I think so, sir, I have been thinking about it, but I'm still not sure. Sometime I wonder if I might become a playwright.'

'It's probably not a bad idea to become a journalist, in view of your passion for writing. I am told by your English teacher that you are writing some excellent essays.'

'I do enjoy writing.'

'I believe it has been estimated that more than 70% of the population over the age of sixteen reads a national newspaper and over 80% read a Sunday paper. The Sunday papers have the biggest readerships of all, especially the trashy *News of the World* and *The People*, and I heard only the other day that these Sundays sell more than 7 million copies between them.'

'Really? I never knew that.'

'But these papers had better make the most of it for as long as they can because, now that television has been invented, millions of readers will not look to them for news in future, they will look to television which will eventually be the nail in the coffin of British newspapers, regionally and nationally very likely. Not that anyone will miss the trashy *News of the World* with all its trashy readers and writers. But right now it would seem that these are halcyon days for tabloid and other newspapers, Robert, so you could probably finish up with a reasonably well-paid job in journalism and a middle-class life and lifestyle go to with it if you work at it.'

'Oh, I do hope so, sir.'

In the fullness of time, Robert finished up living in a very fashionable and glamorous upper-middle class leafy suburb of North London, in a luxury maisonette with a lovely garden, where there was not a working-class community or school in sight, such was his excellent salary and expense account. Like his father before him, he worked hard and long hours, with extra freelance incomes to add to his regular everyday income (as did his secretarial wife, as it happens, a top earner in a global law firm). He had a three-car family and two children – a girl and a boy – whose school fees he paid to private schools. But this was all a long way off and beyond his wildest dreams in 1954.

'But you will have to work at it because it's not as easy as falling off a log for a boy from your background. Most working-class children are encouraged by the educational authority to take modestly paid clerical careers in offices, or to be printers rather than journalists, and most local newspapers in and around this town look down their noses on working-class applicants who want to become newspaper reporters or editors, the vacancies for which are generally regarded to be jobs above their station.'

'So I've heard, sir.'

'First we must see if we cannot get you into university. I have asked Mr McKay to visit your parents and discuss the matter with them without further delay. I would normally have asked your history teacher, Mr Thomas, but he is not every parent's cup of tea, on account of his outspoken communist views, although he is leaving the school shortly to be replaced by a new history teacher called Mr Lacy, who is right of centre, and as for Miss Williams, your class teacher, and Miss Tully, your art teacher, they also tell me good things about you, but they are too new to the school to go and see your parents. And your English teacher, Miss Bone, is unwell at present and likely to remain so for a few weeks, I fear. So I think that Mr McKay is the best person to visit your parents, given that he is the one who has been instrumental in getting your offer from the local Grammar.'

Robert really enjoyed Mr McKay, the geography teacher because he had a wealth of knowledge about the geography of the country and the countryside and what the geophysical and geo-social conditions were in so many different places where towns and cities had developed so very differently, not infrequently on account of their different geographies. This was all very fascinating to Robert, which is why he do so well in his geography exams. There wasn't a town, city or county that one could mention, about which Mr McKay could not tell him all sorts of interesting things, and there wasn't a capital city in the world that Robert couldn't name if asked. Mr McKay was not a former military man, being too young to have fought in World War Two, but he was a disciplinarian for all that, in common with most adults in those days.

Mr McKay told Robert: 'When you go on your long-distance cycling journeys think about the geography of the countryside and how different it is in different places. Think about the difference this makes to the way people live and work in those areas, to the economy in those areas. When you read a map to plot your cycling routes, don't just look at the roads coloured black and red. Think about the other differently shaded colours around those roads and what they are telling you about the geo-physical conditions of the earth in those parts of the country, and then think about how they influence the social and also political conditions. When you look at a map, search for the larger invisible picture in the image of the roads, rivers, hills, mileages and country lanes that you are looking at. When you cycle up a steep hill think about why it is so steep and what it is made of.'

This was all very fascinating indeed to Robert, especially as he was visiting so many places on his bicycle, which is why he particularly enjoyed map-reading lessons and got top marks for them.

Mr McKay had no Scottish accent, but was a chubby-faced Scotsman with a gentle Franciscan monkish sort of expression that was kind and sincere, and he had a lot of time for Robert, as did Mr Thomas, the Welsh history teacher whose moon face was wide open with dark and mischievous eyes that had a twinkle in them. He had a typical Welsh accent (as Jacko Jackson, the Welsh headmaster did not, as we have heard).

Even though Jacko Jackson was absolutely against communism, he still recognised Mr Thomas for the excellent history teacher that he was, and told him 'you can work here, as long as you keep your communist politics to yourself and out of your teaching, as I am sure you will, and as you will be most definitely required to do, make no mistake about that.'

But Mr Thomas did make a very big mistake about that and was instantly fired by Jacko Jackson in consequence. He was not told to bend over and tax six of the best from Jacko's cane, but he was dismissed without further ado.

Robert thought it a pity that Mr Thomas was leaving the school on account of most parents complaining loudly that he was indoctrinating their children with his communist views, which were not very welcome in Britain in the aftermath of World War Two. Robert thought it a pity because Mr Thomas seemed harmless enough and he was a very good history teacher who certainly knew how to provoke thought in his pupils, bringing another interesting political perspective to the interpretation of history, of which students needed to be aware.

As far as Robert was concerned, Mr Thomas was entitled to his opinions and he hadn't succeeded in indoctrinating anyone that Robert could think of, because most children hardly ever listened to him or the other teachers for that matter!

They did not have the IQ or intellect to be indoctrinated!!

On the other hand, Mr Thomas was theoretically in favour of revolution on the streets. But that was only his opinion, he wasn't actively engaged in inciting or organising a revolution, and what was history for, if not to learn from the past and leave no stone unturned when understanding how political and other events came about and why, including communist events?

Robert took the view that opinions had to be listened to, if not agreed with.

But most of the working-class parents at Robert's school were very patriotic and, vociferously so, and they wanted their children to have nothing to do with either communism or fascism after everything they had been through in the war against Nazi Germany, after the threat of communism had brought Hitler to power there.

Even the socialist families had no time for Mr Thomas, who had become a lone voice.

Mr Thomas once told Robert: 'This is supposed to be a free country, yet I am not allowed to have my opinions, same as everybody else in this school. But your history is excellent, Robert. You are consistently top of your class and you show a lot of promise. You have an enquiring mind and you like to challenge things, which is all to the good, and you would do well to study this subject at university if you can get there in this class-dominated country of ours. It's always a pleasure to teach a child who takes a lively interest in his lessons. Makes one think that teaching is worthwhile after all. Sometime I wonder why I bother with most of the kids in this school.'

Robert also wondered why he bothered!

Although Robert enjoyed history enormously, he had thought of studying law or economics at university if he ever got there, but he replied to Mr Thomas that it was a pleasure to be taught by him, which it certainly was, saying that he always looked forward to history lessons, which was perfectly true. Robert was particularly interested in lessons about the British Empire which seemed to have helped itself to a large slice of the world, and to which Mr Thomas objected, naturally, just as he objected to the Queen's Coronation Prize for which Robert was being put forward.

Because Mr Thomas, like royal navy officer Jacko Jackson and also Geoff House a former marine commando physical training teacher (with whom Jacko Jackson sparred in the school gym boxing ring!), were all former World War Two military men – Mr Thomas, a former officer in army intelligence, and Mr House a former sergeant in the commandos – they were predictably no-nonsense and positive teachers, and they were also, each of them, firm but fair disciplinarians, with a high morale and good team spirit that they brought with them from their respective military and wartime backgrounds. They knew the importance of high morale and how to demonstrate it and they seldom if at all let things get them down and certainly not out of hand.

Their morale and team spirit brushed off on many of their pupils and not least on Robert. Whilst they did not take any nonsense from disruptive pupils, of whom there were many, they went out of their way to play to the strengths and weaknesses of all their pupils, treating them all fairly and squarely and finding practical ways of helping the less able to learn what they could not otherwise learn academically, encouraging them to believe in themselves for whatever it was that they could do, and to make the most of themselves on account of it.

They sang from the same song sheet and usually said: 'Whatever it is that you can do, get on and do it well. If you can only do a little, then make sure that you do a little well, very well indeed. Whatever it is that you can do – only a little or a lot – do it well and it will be the making of you in one way or another.'

Robert thought that many of the working-class parents and their children were their own worst enemies, being so ignorantly opposed to education and also so very disruptive and aggressively quarrelsome with it – which is why he had no time for them and hardly ever socialised with them or dated their young women or school girls (he dated, instead, grammar school and fee-paying private school girls in the town and got to know them and their parents very well).

Mr Thomas told Robert: 'The reason why this school is such a dump is because all the working-class kids who failed their eleven-plus examinations have been dumped here without any intention of or need for them to be educated further before they leave school, when they take an apprenticeship for whichever trade they opt for when they leave. So they do not of course need a higher education and this is saving tax payers' moneys to the tune of millions if not billions of pounds, which suits the government very well.'

Robert already knew this very well of course.

'As for the outrageous 11-plus exam,' Mr Thomas continued, ' it's not a fair or equal contest between those who pass it and those who fail, because the latter are in no way properly prepared for it by their parents in their homes before they take it – and certainly not in most of the state junior schools that they attend – whereas the former certainly are properly prepared for it in either or both of those places, since their junior schools are in socially better and more affluent neighbourhoods with the more intelligent children of professional parents who can afford to live there, people who take education more seriously and more seriously value it, making sure to prepare their children for this exam in their homes.'

From his own experience, Robert knew perfectly well that Mr Tomas had put his finger on the sensitive nature of the problem, but what best to do about it?

Mr Thomas was a 'reliable narrator' in his view, not that those who turned a deaf ear and a blind eye to him wanted to admit this. They denied and challenged what he said, either because they could not stand him, or because they had too much to lose by agreeing with him.

If they had managed to pass the 11-plus, they had face to lose by admitting that it was an unfair and/or stupid exam, that they had had an unfair advantage that others did not have.

And if the exam needed to be replaced, to allow
for the education of more children, they had all the upheaval and tax payers' money of all that
to lose at great financial and also political cost.

So there really was too much to lose all round.

Better to deny and ignore what Mr Thomas and so many other critics like him in this regard – not all communists by any stretch of the imagination -
were saying, better to dismiss it and him out of hand.

But Mr Thomas was adamant that: 'The whole system stinks, which is why I come to school with a peg on my nose in order to teach here.'

Whilst Robert – he and his parents - were far from being communists, like Mr Thomas, they did not disagree with his explanation. On account of Robert and his brothers having been in no way suitably or properly prepared for this exam when they took it, they could hardly disagree, not that Robert's mother thought that it mattered very much, given that she was in favour of children leaving school early and earning some much-needed money for the homes from which they came.

Robert had not even heard of the exam until after he had taken it – he just turned up at junior school one morning and was given some exam papers without knowing what they were for!

He thought that they must be for some internal test, not for an external competitive examination with long-term consequences for his education, which is almost certainly why he and his two brothers had failed it, not that this had deterred the local grammar school from offering at least one of them – Robert – a place as soon as it recognised (thanks to Mr McKay) that he was more than capable of making the grade required of him.

There had been no swotting or homework for this exam, no preparation of any kind.

Mr Thomas added: 'What is the point of getting kids in junior schools in these parts to sit an exam for which they have not been prepared and of which many if not most of them have never heard? How stupid is that? What is the point of giving them an exam to sit that they do not know they are sitting? It is of course an outrageous con. Most kids in this school are sledge-hammered with the heavy boredom of education of any kind, and never mind a higher education in which they and most of their parents have zero interest. These parents send their kids to school for others to get them off their hands and discipline them. Discipline is all that matters in this school, not education or a fair chance of getting an education, except for the odd pupil like you Robert. All that education means in this school is caning kids and keeping them in order, not teaching them kindly or intelligently, but telling them to put up and shut up and do as they're told – regimenting them socially and for the armed forces as and when needed.'

Because there were was no shortage of male teachers who had inevitably done military wartime and also colonial service in the 1950s - as had many if not most of the fathers of the children attending the school - it followed from this that these children were well regimented, as observed by Mr Thomas, from the cradle and, with common consent, they were all expected to be disciplined and respectful to each other and to their elders, parents and school teachers. Those recalcitrants that failed this expectation were swiftly dealt with, not that this stopped them from persistently seeking to disrupt their classes and disrespect their teachers on account of their boredom, and also of their resentment of any other children who did not share their boredom.

A child could not get to the end of the street in which he or she lived without one of the neighbours interfering and asking where it thought it was going, what it was 'up to,' why it wasn't at school etc. and giving a boy 'a thick ear' if he dared to be cheeky or answer back! Every move that children and adults made in those days was carefully watched by neighbours, street sweepers, post men, bin men, milk men, delivery men and so on, all of whom came together in the common cause of disciplining their communities and making sure that they were orderly and law-abiding – disciplining one and all and making no exception for unruly children, who behave as if it was their only purpose in life – to be unruly as they had been born and reared to be!

But it was a pity that Miss Bone the English teacher was not well, because she was more likely to win Robert's mother round in order to get him off to the local grammar, more than Mr McKay and most of the other teachers (not that Robert cared for Miss Bone very much or even at all!).

A former – failed – opera singer with grandly permed, very shiny silvery-grey hair, the presumably lower-middle-class Miss Bone (why else was she in the school?) was an impressive physical character, strikingly buxom and bosomy, perfumed and scented to go with it, and very snooty and snobby to boot, and she had the kind of grandly exaggerated English accent of which Robert did not approve.

The handsome and authoritarian Miss Bone was posh at a time in British history when you had to be posh (at least in quotes) in order to be taken seriously. You had to have a posh accent, a posh appearance and a posh job, the latter being dependent to a large extent on the former. And Miss Bone had a posh silver-grey, blue-tinted and regularly permed hairstyle to go with it, a hairstyle that she wore like a glittering crown!

Like Queen Elizabeth II's tiara.

Robert thought that Miss Bone and the Queen of England both sounded as though they had taken very strict elocution lessons daily and stage-managed them, as they respectively 'put on' their very stiff and wooden 'royal' accents that were grandly designed to impress and put others in their place and keep them there (down there!), as they 'talked down' to people, rather like High Court Judges.

Whilst a posh voice did not equate with intelligence necessarily, it gave the not infrequently false impression that one must be intelligent!

Unlike later on in history, there was no way in early 1950s Britain in Robert's home town and so many others like it that anybody with a grass-roots accent - or who was not well spoken and smartly dressed - was going to get ahead (which is why Robert had polished up his own country accent, but not in such an exaggerate and affected way, he had only poshed his accent up a little!).

Even Mr Thomas's typical Welsh accent, was an educated and literate accent.

Being a former officer in the Royal Navy, Robert's headmaster was certainly posh – one could not have become an officer and a gentleman in the Senior Service otherwise – but he was not overly and absurdly posh, like Miss Bone. He was sort of effortlessly posh, whilst she was studiously posh and always 'putting it on' in the opinion of Robert's father who, with his broad country accent, could tell the difference between real posh and fake or contrived posh.

With his posh and commanding accent – and his cane! - Jacko Jackson knew exactly how to deal with a class of obstinately uncooperative and stubborn, very recalcitrant schoolboys opposed to receiving a 'fancy' education, and also dealing with their fathers if they dared to intervene, as some of them often did, in their attempts to intimidate him and his teachers.

But Robert's mother was a very different problem, which is why it would have been better to send Miss Bone to see her, had she not been ill.

As a former failed-opera-singer, Miss Bone had great presence, and she was exactly the kind of woman that featured in romantic fiction of the kind that Robert's mother liked to read – well-groomed and impeccably dressed, refined, lady-like and glamorous (her silvery grey, permanently permed hair, was shot through with the bluest of blue tints and was quite a spectacle).

Miss Bone was a big woman who talked with a big plum in her mouth and she had a proud and haughty demeanour with a self-satisfied face that somehow also managed to look naturally serene, as she looked down on people (for fear of otherwise having to look up to them!).

No doubt about it, she was, with her famously unforgettable blue-rinse, silver grey hair, the teacher most likely to impress Robert's mother, to whom appearances were all-important, and what was more it was rumoured that Miss Bone was married to a professional man who was reportedly very well off.

She lived in a large corner house that suggested that she and her husband were a cut above their neighbours whose terrace houses were much smaller and had much smaller gardens, and it was a mystery to those neighbours what a former opera singer was doing, slumming with her posh accent and professional husband, slumming in a working-class school, with an accent that was in direct contrast to the country accents of her children and their parents.

Nobody knew or asked outright, because that would have been far too impolite!

Of the three Welsh teachers in the school, Mr Thomas had the most pronounced and obvious Welsh accent of which he was very proud, whilst the head master, Jacko Jackson, had a very English accent, and Robert's class teacher, Miss Williams' Welsh accent was gentle and soft.

Miss Bone once told Robert, in her excessively posh accent and with an undisguised sneer that was so condescending and supercilious that it suggested that she thought that he was far beneath her (as indeed he was, socially speaking, but not otherwise): 'Your writing is very imaginative, but you must pay more attention to your spelling. I expect your spelling reflects the way your parents mispronounce their words and the fact that you have no dictionary in your home. That's what you told me, isn't it, that you do not have a dictionary in your home?'

This was true of Robert's home at the time, but as soon as Robert's mother heard of Miss Bone sneering about this, she consented to a dictionary being bought.

'Yes, that's right miss. And my parents do mispronounce too many words, but my mother gets the majority of them right most of the time. It's just that, when they make a mistake, it's a real howler, and everybody remembers it and has a good laugh, but nobody remembers all the other words with which they are familiar, that my parents do use and pronounce correctly, which is more than you can say for quite a lot of people in our neighbourhood. The thing is, miss, my parents left school at 11 and 12 years of age.'

This was true. Robert's parents took care to listen carefully to how well-spoken people spoke English and to copy them, as a result of which his father – with his unashamed country accent – could quite often speak grammatically, as could his wife, who had also made the effort to get rid of her working-class country accent. But Robert's father could not write grammatically and he could not spell. Nor had he attempted to get rid of his accent. Robert's parents had learnt their English by rote, not from English teachers or books in classrooms. And they learnt the meanings of words by word of mouth, by what other people told them the words meant, taking care to find out from the people who were most likely to know, such as relatives who were sufficiently well educated to get jobs in offices, rather than menial or labouring jobs, and from travelling and insurance salesmen who called at the house and spoke correctly. There were a lot of door-to-door salesmen in those days. So Robert's parents picked up figures of speech and copied them if they sounded right, and Robert's mother - who read a lot of contemporary novels of a romantic or murderous kind (detective stories) - spoke as the characters in her novels spoke. Once in a while Robert's parents got a word completely wrong, having taken its meaning on trust from somebody who didn't know what they were talking about, and other times they used words in the wrong context. Here was an English working-class couple – typical of a great many - who were like foreigners to their own native tongue.

Let's not forget that when Robert's parents were teenagers in the early 20th century, when they put on their 'Sunday best' clothes once a week and went for a stroll through the town's high street on Sunday afternoons or evenings, to look in the shop windows there - when they did this, the working classes to which they belonged kept to one side of the road where all the working-class shops were, while the middle and upper classes kept to the other side where all the posh shops were – as both social groups stared at each other from a distance across the divide, without having any social contact or mutual regard whatsoever.

Had a working-class person crossed the road, to look into the windows of the posh shops, he or she would very soon have been told to stop being pretentious - looking into stores at which they could not possibly afford to shop and where their custom would not have been welcome - and to get back to the scruffy side of the street from which they came!

This was white-on-white apartheid.

No doubt Miss Bone's parents and grandparents would have been among them!

Or if they would not have been, there was nothing about Miss Bone to suggest otherwise in her snooty and condescending attitude to Robert and his parents.

'Your parents probably cannot help using words,' Miss Bone continued, 'the meanings of which they do not understand. It's very common where you live,' and she said this as if she were taking some kind of revenge on him and his kind.

Robert did not disagree with this – or that he needed to work at his spelling (in due course he became a near-perfect speller) – but he replied 'they do sometimes, but they also understand quite a lot of words.'

Having learnt the English language by ear - like some people learn how to play music without being able to read the notes – the English that Robert's parents used was not unmusical (or un-comical!), unlike the Queen of England's unmusical and comical English that was stilted and uptight, with its tortured and tight-lipped vowel sounds that were so tightly controlled and restrained through her tight lips that it seemed to many that she hardly opened her mouth at all. Her speech was so wooden and splintery (and this, too, was not un-comical!).

Whilst Robert's family spoke grammatically, much of the time, if one tested their grammar with a lot of questions about it, they would fail the test miserably. If you asked them what a preposition was, they wouldn't have a clue. Yet they managed to speak most of their sentences without ending them with prepositions, because that's what they heard people doing on the radio in the days when standard Oxford/BBC English was the norm on the radio. But when it came to spelling, they were all over the place, quite unable to make up their minds whether there should be one or two Ms in summer, that sort of thing, etc. etc. And they did not usually bother with apostrophes because they could never remember where to put them, not having been taught this very simple rule, which was hardly rocket science, but which can be mildly confusing if you don't know what the rule is. It was not that they were too lazy to bother with apostrophes – as many people certainly were and are to this day - but that they didn't mess with things they didn't understand.

Robert told Miss Bone: 'My father never swears, because my mother would not allow him in the house if he were to do so.' He could have added to this that he never discusses sex in the house, either, because that too was a taboo subject with Robert's mother! The house was a sex-free zone with no references to it, let alone open discussions about it.

Miss Bone smiled quietly to her self-satisfied self. She knew the street where Robert and his parents lived and she did not think much of it – nor did Robert for that matter! - which is doubtless why her favourite pupils did not come from that street, which was at the wrong end of town and a lot tougher and rougher, by far, than other working-class and lower-middle class streets in the area.

The middle-aged and middle-class Miss Bone was a condescending cow, smoothly self-assured and incredibly unruffled. She walked as if she was walking on water –

gliding over it. Whilst she was a handsome woman, she had never been too feminine or sexy – also important to Robert's mother who did not approve of women being too openly or obviously feminine or sexy! – and she was, on the face of it, a model of perfection, with elocution and vowel sounds that were as perfect as her appearance. Some of the children joked that she must have secretly thought that she was the Queen of England.

But in Robert's view, Miss Bone's great failing as a teacher was that she had her favourites, and since her favourites did not always succeed as she imagined that they would, this suggested that her judgement was not exactly kosher (not that Miss Bone would ever use such a vulgar word as kosher).

Robert was not, alas, one of Miss Bone's favourites, and she had her doubts about him as a person because she preferred schoolboys who were lap dogs, born to be charmed by the Miss Bones of this world, as Robert's mother was certainly charmed by the carefully modulated voice of perfectly groomed Miss Bone.

But Miss Bone's reservations about Robert did not mean that she could not grudgingly acknowledge his good work, with which she let it be known that she was reasonably impressed - with certain reservations naturally – or that she could deny that he had potential for higher education. Her reservations about him centred on his personality and class background, not on his work.

Robert's personality was not sufficiently subservient for Miss Bone, not sufficiently in awe of her, not sufficiently po-faced, and he had a confident and mischievous grin that unnerved her. Not being full of smiles herself, Miss Bone found grinning faces distasteful!

Whilst Robert was never impolite or disrespectful to her, there was no way that he made it obvious that he looked up to her, as she made it obvious that she looked down on him.

Mr Thomas told Robert that the middle and/or lower-middle classes, from which Miss Bone came, felt more threatened by the working classes, and that they felt this much more than those above them in the upper classes. This was because - as the buffer between the upper and the rock-bottom lower - the middle, especially the lower middle, were too close for comfort to the working classes and were in fact inevitably much more threatened by them, which made the middle feel uncomfortable. Which is why, he argued, they needed to put on so many airs and graces in order to distance themselves more than the upper classes - who couldn't be more naturally distant and secure if they tried - so they were not threatened and had no need of distancing themselves. For this reason, Mr Thomas reckoned that the lower middle could be much more snobbish towards the working classes than the upper classes who were only dimly aware of the existence of the working classes!

As for monarchy, Mr Thomas had no time for such a quaint institution whatsoever and would like to see it abolished.

But the only thing that was being abolished was Mr Thomas!

He who was being driven out of the school by working-class parents, most of whom did not want to see monarchy abolished, and did not want him bending their children's ear on the subject of a communist revolution or the virtues of communism.

Probably he would go to a working-class school on a council estate somewhere where the parents were trades unionists and had no objection to his extreme political views.

Unlike today, because times were so much harder, the class system and its politics were a regular topic of conversation in 1950s Britain where young people could not grow up without a very clear awareness of the class to which they belonged, with or without an inferiority or superiority complex to go with it.

Robert was completely without any such ridiculous thing as an inferiority or superiority complex and he frequently said so, and this did not appeal to Miss Bone either, as she certainly expected the working classes to know their place and to wear their inferiority complexes like a badge or a health warning of some kind! Identifiable working-class accents and inferiority complexes were music to her ears, because they made her feel superior, and Robert's neutrality in this regard certainly unnerved her. The only inferiority that was bothering Robert was the inferior education on offer at his school, which is why he wanted out at the first opportunity, wanted a transfer to the grammar school at the first opportunity.

Whilst he rated most of his school teachers highly – they were doing a good job, the best they could do in the lowly circumstances – he did not rate the other pupils in the school, or indeed their parents, most of whom were anti-education, which is why standards in the school were so low and why, by contrast, his standards were so effortlessly high. He wanted to be with other more intelligent and more serious pupils. He wanted competition from them and also their company.

To have a personality compatible with Miss Bone's – as Robert did not - meant that your face had to fit and that one had to be something of a toady. She had to like the colour of your eyes and you had to be the kind of man or boy who was not his own man or boy, but Miss Bone's man or boy. But all the queenly Miss Bone had to do was to condescend to tell Robert's mother that her son could go far at university and – who knows? – Miss Bone's magical aura and presence (in the mind of Robert's mother in her humble home) may win his mother round. Miss Bone could not honestly say that Robert was not university material, now that the head and the other teachers were backing him.

Robert's favourite female teachers were his art teacher, Miss Tully, about whom he had sexual fantasies, and his class teacher, Miss Williams (who taught drama among other things), both of whom would doubtless be too young (i.e. immature!) and too pretty and sexually attractive for his mother's liking.

Miss Tully could tell that Robert fancied her from, as usual, the way that he looked at her, and she once brushed his fringe from his eyes, saying: 'You need to cut this fringe of yours, Robert, it's getting in your eyes too much.'

It was highly unusual for Robert's fringe to be falling into his eyes because his mother regularly dragged him to the barber – a local Polish gentleman who fled to England when Hitler invaded Poland – for what was popularly known as a short-back-and-sides *basin haircut* (basin on the head, all hair sliced off around the sides and beneath the upturned basin looking like a helmet!).

Most schoolboys were regimented by their parents into keeping their hair short, which had to be flattened and stuck firmly to their heads with smelly-sweet *Brylcreem*, a white sticky substance that Robert hated because he was in favour of natural long hair, hanging loose. The object of the creem/cream was to hold the hair firmly in place, stick it there and give it a shine and also a sickly smell, preventing fringes from falling into one's eyes. But Miss Tully had caught Robert on a day when he had washed his hair and had deliberately neglected to stick it down. 'You are a good-looking boy,' she told him, 'but this fringe is getting out of control.'

It wasn't only the fringe over Robert's forehead that was getting out of control when Miss Tully was around!

Robert hadn't had any sexual fantasies about Miss Williams yet, but he intended to do so in due course, after he was through with Miss Tully.

He liked both these teachers very much, especially Miss Tully who warmed to him as a person and frequently invited him to stay on after school and help her tidy up the art room, putting the differently coloured crayons back into the huge floor-to-ceiling, walk-in cupboard, in which all the art materials were kept. She seemed to enjoy Robert's company and he was only too pleased to assist her tidying up the classroom after school when everyone had gone home.

As for Miss Williams, she wrote Robert good reports: 'A natural leader in his class. Takes great pride in his personal appearance. A quiet boy – but not in the school playground! – who works well at his subjects. A very bright boy who should go far.'

With his mother on his back, Robert had no choice but to take great pride in his personal appearance. Children were undeniably relatively poor, but they had to be scrubbed clean and smartly turned out at all times, smelling strongly of rosy-red Carbolic soap and sickly *Brylcreem.*

Yet –to return to the subject of class snobbery in society – there was an educated and well-spoken boy who lived in a nearby middle-class neighbourhood that was very refined, who insisted on nicknaming Robert 'Scruffy' whenever he came across him in the local park, not because Robert was scruffy, but because this boy always wanted to remind him that he came from the scruffy end of town, where all the children were supposedly scruffs and always would be. However clean and smartly turned out one or two of them may be, like Robert, they would always be scruffs in this boy's highly prejudiced middle-class view, which he had no doubt acquired from his parents and neighbours, and he was typical of many others of his kind.

On one occasion, this boy pushed his luck too far, 'hello Scruffy, back in this lovely park again, I see. I would have thought you'd be more at home playing with all the scruffy kids in the scruffy back streets where you live.'

To which Robert replied, 'in that case, have a scruffy punch on the nose and see how you like it,' as he punched the boy smack on his nose and made it bleed, as a result of which the boy fled at once and did not bother Robert again.

Robert always stood up to bullies in his school and his life – he never bullied anyone himself, but he never ceased to stand up to bullies when they came his way – and he told himself that this child was a middle-class verbal and psychological bully who deserved his nose bleed.

The teachers that Robert least liked were the commerce teacher, Mr Marler, who had a permanently inane grin on his face, and permanently bad breath. He was a former army sergeant who did not hesitate to smack the backs of boys' legs – by hand or with a ruler - for disobeying him, or merely for forgetting to do things. He was popularly known as 'dog's breath.'

Robert wasn't too keen on Mr Wyatt, either. He was a tall, balding man, with a drooping moustache, who taught metalwork and woodwork – the two subjects that bored Robert out of his mind - and when Robert asked him if he could not devote more time to his English, History or Geography instead of wasting time on metalwork and woodwork, he echoed the headmaster's old familiar words that, 'in this life we have to do a lot of things that we don't like or want to do, and the sooner you learn this the better' (play another record!).

As for Robert's German teacher, Mr Baxter, he was a supply teacher, and such an anodyne character that he made hardly impression at all, although he did manage to get a goodly amount of the German language into Robert's head (for some reason, there was no French teacher, probably a supply teacher could not be found for such a school that could not or would not afford full-time foreign language teachers).

So Robert was glad that it was Mr McKay - in the absence of Miss Bone, as we have heard- who was coming to see Robert's parents about getting him into the local grammar school and off university.

How exciting!

And what is more, Robert was now off to W.H.Smith with his book tokens, even more exciting!

Chapter Four: Robert's Choice of Books

So Robert was about to be on his way to choose his prize with his book tokens!

Twenty-seven million books had been sold in England at the beginning of World War Two – three times more than ten years previously – and a gentleman called Sir Allen Lane, of whom Robert had heard nothing, had published his first sixpenny paperbacks before the second world war, yet not one of these had found its way into Robert's home, where pennies were scraped together in order to survive, and sixpence was not to be wasted on printed words.

Sir Allen Lane became very famous indeed, especially for his Penguin Books that in the fullness of time became a national and global brand.

Reading books and publishing them was chiefly a middle-class habit, cultivated, financed and encouraged by the middle classes, the upper-middle in particular.

But there were always cheaper comics for the working and lower middle classes, especially the *Dandy*, *Beano* and a publication called *Boys Own Paper*, and Robert also had it in mind to publish a paper of his own one day soon, to be entitled *Youth's Own Paper (YOP)*. This was another aspect of his public spiritedness, but its launch came a couple of years after his Coronation Prize was awarded to him, and too late to win any extra feathers in his cap with those educational and other worthies that judged him for the prize (their protected identity was a mystery to Robert, it was said to be protected to avoid any favouritism by reason of candidates or their parents bringing influence or pressure to bear).

Robert's paper - a magazine, as it turned out - had to be entitled *YOP* because when he first launched it as the *Voice of Youth*, he soon got a letter from the Poetry Society's lawyers in London telling him that the Society had copyrighted the title, *Voice of Youth*, for itself, so he would have to change the name, which is how and why *YOP* became his second choice.

It was a local commercial artist who suggested *YOP* to Robert when he drew him an image of a roly-poly, mischievous little sausage of a dog called *YOP!*

Robert went to see this artist - a kindly old man living in a bungalow overlooking the River Thames that ran through the town where Robert lived - who had been recommended to Robert. 'the schoolboy publisher (!!),' by a grammar school friend who suggested that this nice old man would probably have plenty of ideas and may even do an image without charge, which he did.

He was a very successful commercial artist who invented *Mr Cube* – the popular sugar cube on the packets of Tate & Lyle sugar and it was he who swiftly came up with the idea of *YOP* for *Youth's Own Paper*.

Various celebrities sent good-luck and congratulatory letters to Robert that he published in his paper, including one from the famous pop-singer Frankie Vaughan in Liverpool who did a lot of work with and for the National Association of Youth Clubs (his autographed photo appeared on the front cover of *Voice of Youth* before its name-change), as well as the famous actress Sylvia Syms (who was featured in the inside editorial pages for her various films, one of which was called *A Town Like Alice*, in which she co-starred with John Mills).

These were all very notable, famous and helpful people in 1950s England, who did not hesitate to give Robert a leg up, as soon as they heard about his efforts - his having been interviewed in his home on BBC Radio to begin with, prior to the launch of his magazine (but with a printed sample copy to show them, printed by a local printer called Jack Stein who very helpfully told Robert that he was in no hurry for payment during the initial start-up of his publication), and then on television after its launch.

Sally Belfrage, newly arrived from the United States, was a young aspiring journalist who had been to Moscow to attend a Youth Festival there, but had stayed on for a year and written and published a best-selling paperback book about it, entitled *A Room in Moscow,* that Robert reviewed in his fledgling publication. An unheard of trade union young man called Arthur Scargill had also attended this festival in Moscow when nobody had any idea of who he was or what a notorious leader he would become,

A Young aspiring actor called Robert Bridges wrote for Robert's publications because Robert wanted to give a voice to the youth in his town and his country, of whom Robert Bridges was one.

For this new generation of war babies and their successors - of whom Robert was one - this working-class lad, who had been born on Sept 11, 1939 at the outbreak of war with not a single book in his home (not even a dictionary to begin with, or an encyclopaedia or bible later on), persuaded the town's local university students, together with student nurses in nurses' homes, to help him distribute his publication). There was something about him and his charisma, to which they all responded, and never mind his having come from the 'scruffy' end of town.

As we see, Robert was nothing if not very enterprising for one so young and he produced his brain child in the upstairs' attic bedroom of the terrace house in which he was born and reared.

But this was all in the near future in the wake of his Coronation Prize, not before it or immediately after it, and not before he had collected his book tokens from the Queen of England.

Before he took leave of Jacko Jackson to go and choose his books, Jacko said to him: 'Before you go, I just want to tell you a little about the history of the W.H. Smith bookshop, as I imagine that you don't know anything about it.'

'Nothing at all, sir.'

'The shop has sent us a little pamphlet which explains that it got started a very long time ago, back in 1792 when Henry Walter Smith founded his newsagents in London. He was succeeded by his son, William Henry Smith, and the company had the foresight to take advantage of Britain's railway boom, following the very first railways wherever they went, and opening newsagents at all the stations where the new steam trains were dropping their passengers and where station hotels were being built, starting at Euston Station in 1848.'

'Very enterprising of them, sir.'

Talking of hotels, the Station Hotel in Station Road in Robert's home town was generally regarded as the grandest that the town had to offer, back in the 1940s and 1950s, and it was predictably very snobby for this reason. Working-class people kept well away from this no-go hotel, from which they were turned away when some occasionally dared to go anywhere near it, which was why, within a few years of being entered for his Coronation Prize, Robert was determined to make a little working-class history by taking himself into the hotel and buying himself a drink in the bar there. His father told him that, as a working-class lad, he would not be welcome there, and his mother said that the hotel doorman would not allow him across the threshold. But, undeterred, Robert scrubbed himself up, put on his best suit of clothes and his best Oxford/BBC accent – unlike his father, he had very deliberately not acquired a broad country accent, as we have heard - and took himself off to the hotel to see if he could prove his parents wrong and show the way by breaking the class barrier.

He had saved just enough six penny pieces and shillings to buy himself a drink in the hotel bar and he was determined not to fall foul of the white on white apartheid that was operated there. As bold as brass, he walked up to the doorman and asked him: 'Where is the bar, my good man? I'm new to this town and hotel, but have heard that you have an excellent bar?'

No doubt thinking that Robert was the son of a wealthy toff, the doorman was only too pleased to let Robert pass as he directed him to the bar!

The country town in which Robert grew up had a squirearchy at the top of its society and also a lot of pretentious middle-class types who generally sucked up to them, whilst the working class majority – out of sight and out of mind on the council estates and in the back streets – usually avoided them like the plague because they did not have the self-belief and the self-confidence, or the education or the money, to go among them and hold their own with them on equal terms. But Robert clearly had the cheek (minus the money!) from a very young age.

These class barriers existed all over Britain where there was a kind of truce between the two sides that did their best to ignore each other. But before long – in the late 1950s and 1960s – there would be a massive sea change in British society and culture that would sweep away these class tensions and divisions, once and for all, ushering in a meritocracy and a new social order, in place of the old aristocracy and squirearchy, most of whom had previously not got ahead on merit, and had tried to pretend that the lower orders either did not exist or, if they did, that they had not merit at all!

But the new social order that replaced them by Robert and his kind would be driven by new economic and political forces that were pretty much unimaginable to Robert's parents and neighbours in the early 1950s, and also driven by an increase in much improved education for the masses in the long march of time. But Robert was ahead of his time, because he was getting himself reasonably well educated long before improved education was available for the masses.

He was nicknamed 'long word Charlie' by many of the less intelligent boys in his school because he had an advanced vocabulary and was learning, using and correctly spelling so many words that others did not bother to learn themselves. Any words that he came across, for which he did not know the meanings, he made a note of them and looked them up in the dictionary that eventually found its way into his home. So he was quite articulate for one so young and from his disadvantaged background. But his detractors referred to him as a 'proper Charlie' because, in their opinion, he took himself too seriously on account of having swallowed a dictionary, and was too wordy and full of himself on account of all the words he knew.

A 'Charlie' was a person that was supposed to be too full of himself. Actually, Robert did not take himself seriously at all and was not too full of himself, but because he took language seriously and respected words, many of the other boys misunderstood him and were out of sympathy with him (as he was certainly out of sympathy with them).

'It was, as you say, very enterprising indeed,' the head replied to Robert, with previous reference to WH Smith, 'because they made an absolute fortune and were soon raised high in British society. They were able to grow their nationwide newsagents into a chain of bookshops, not for highbrows or academics, but for readers of popular-interest books. William Henry Smith became the First Lord of the Admiralty and was duly satirised by Gilbert & Sullivan in their opera *H.M.S. Pinafore.*'

'Satirised, sir?' (this is how Robert learnt so many new words, he always asked what they meant, or otherwise looked them up in his dictionary that he did not have when Miss Bone was being sneery about it!).

'Mickey-taking, boy! Satire is taking the mickey.'

'Oh, I see. But not the Charlie!'

'Very good, Robert, very witty.'

Because this was early 1950s Britain, in the decade before the *Pythons* and the televised satire boom of the 1960s, with David Frost and *That Was The Week That Was*, few if any people had heard of satire or knew anything about it. They may even have thought it was some kind of disease or illness!

This was a Britain in which there was not much taking the mickey, and certainly not of the upper classes by the lower classes. There was the *Goon Show* on steam radio, as already mentioned, which was more clowning around than seriously satirical, let alone political mickey-taking, and Robert never failed to miss this programme.

'Yes, well,' the head continued, 'I thought you should know just a little about this amazing bookshop, which has 280 library branches nationwide with some 60,000 subscribers. These are its own library shops where you can borrow books for a small membership fee, if you cannot afford to buy them. So perhaps you see from this brief history why this shop's book tokens are being used by the Queen of England for this prize of hers, a prize that she is giving to you personally. This is an extraordinary shop for an extraordinary prize.'

'Yes, it is, isn't it?'

To which the head replied: 'Off you go then, Robert, and look smart about it. Have you decided yet which kind of books you are likely to choose?'

'I have heard from Mr McKay that W.H.Smith may have a book called *100 Great Lives* and another that is the *Oxford University Road Atlas of Britain* and, if so, I will give these books a try, as they sound very interesting.'
'They do indeed, Robert, they sound like an excellent choice to me.'

Whereupon, Robert went on his way.

This is the end of part-one of this sequel, readers can order part-two in time for the New Year 2023 by going online at mxpublishing.com or requesting this book on Amazon or in the book shops.